Sunbeams, Butt

Also by Chris Page

Bright Lights and Fairy Dust

Sunbeams, Butterflies and Feathers

Matters of Life after Death

Chris Page

Grosvenor House
Publishing Limited

All rights reserved
Copyright © Chris Page, 2018

The right of Chris Page to be identified as the author of this
work has been asserted in accordance with Section 78
of the Copyright, Designs and Patents Act 1988

The book cover picture is copyright to Chris Page

This book is published by
Grosvenor House Publishing Ltd
Link House
140 The Broadway, Tolworth, Surrey, KT6 7HT.
www.grosvenorhousepublishing.co.uk

This book is sold subject to the conditions that it shall not, by way of
trade or otherwise, be lent, resold, hired out or otherwise circulated
without the author's or publisher's prior consent in any form of binding or
cover other than that in which it is published and
without a similar condition including this condition being imposed
on the subsequent purchaser.

A CIP record for this book
is available from the British Library

ISBN 978-1-78623-405-6

The conversations in this book come from the author's recollections
and may not, therefore, be word-for-word transcripts. The author has
written them in a way that communicates the feeling and meaning of
what was said and in every case, the essence of the dialogue is accurate.

In order to maintain their anonymity in some instances, for literary effect,
the names of individuals have been changed. Identifying characteristics
may also have been changed and the reader should not consider
this book anything other than a work of literature.

Nothing in this book is intended to be interpreted as giving medical
advice of any nature whatsoever or as being a substitute for seeking a
medical opinion from qualified professionals.

In loving memory,
Linda
and
Pa

*'A single sunbeam is enough
to drive away many shadows'*

Francis of Assisi

Contents

Acknowledgements

Sunbeams, Butterflies and Feathers is an expression of gratitude to all my family, my friends and the many people I have met on my continuing voyage. It would be difficult, if not impossible, to name them all in this short book, but every person who has come into my life has in some way helped me on my way and I am forever grateful for their healing kindness.

I thank the professionals who have helped me with counselling and the various health issues I have had since Linda's passing.

Thank you to the staff of the Duchess of Kent Hospice for the care and help I received after Linda died. And to Dennis, John, Michael, Jim, Cathy, Yvonne, Chris, Jenny and Jennie, our coffee mornings were always a source of support for me and I value your friendship.

Within the Writers Group, Kate, Chris and Lou have given me encouragement and constructive comment as I have tried to convert my jottings, notes and journal entries into the body of text between the covers of this book.

My thanks also go to the many members of the clergy and the congregations with whom I have engaged, for your support, love and care, and for my Confirmation, all of which continues to give me strength.

I am grateful to members of the bands *Mo Cairde* and *Inisheer* and to *Craig Folk*, to your wives, husbands, partners and everyone with whom I sing and play, for your love and patience and for encouraging me back to the music. It has proved to be a great motivator.

To Ric and Maggie; Sarah and Robert; Fiona; Ian and Kathy; Deirdre and Leroy; Fran and Carl; John and Leonie; Auntie Hilda; Tony and Maria, your warm hospitality and continued support means much to me and I thank you for putting me up (or putting up with me) when I visited.

When my father went into heart block, Doctor Sandhu's quick thinking saved his life and we are all grateful beyond measure. Thank you, Sandy.

I am blessed that my Darling Linda continues to be a tower of strength for me. I have only to reach out to her; she is never far away.

My eternal love and thanks to Wayne, Sara, Lola and Darcy for supporting me every step of the way. I know you hurt too, but there is strength in numbers and it's *'the six of us, together'* now. We will carry on.

Introduction

These days, it's not often that I write a letter.

I know my email and computer have changed the way I write, but at Christmas I used to pen a long distance catch up letter to our friends in the City of Blue Mountains, New South Wales.

Just a week after Linda's visit to the doctor, I wrote to them and, as with every letter I sent on behalf of us both, I let Linda read it before tucking it inside their Christmas card and sealing the envelope.

East Fields
December

There is no easy way for anyone to announce that cancer is about to claim the life of a loved one, but I open this letter with the news that Linda has been diagnosed with a tumour. It's been a hectic week and a half, of doctors' visits, blood tests, chest x-ray and (yesterday) a CT scan, all of which conclude that my Darling wife has a large, inoperable cancer on her right lung.

Because no one had the slightest idea this would happen, we have received many Christmas cards wishing us a good time and a happy new year.

Christmas has always evoked memories of loved ones lost. This Christmas, it's about a loved one to be lost because we know this may be our last together.

I'm sorry to bear such heavy news, but we have to let people know so that we can be strong in the coming months.

We've worked hard on this house over the past seven and a half years and I now sit and wonder what it was all for. Linda says, 'We did it. I can see now what we always dreamed of and I love what we've done. I have no regrets.' Linda is just amazing and I am in her shadow.

Although my letter has brought such terrible news, I do hope that you all have a good Christmas. We'll be thinking of you, as we always do, and I will cherish, as I always will, all those special moments with you all.

Love and best wishes to everyone,
Chris, Linda, Wayne and Sara
xxxx

fter ten hard months of fighting, Linda's journey was over.

However, because we had always thought of it as 'our cancer', I was still on the road, alone now, my destination shrouded in mist. Although, hour by hour, I was able to place my feet, I couldn't see where I was going.

And I didn't *know* where I was going.

When I was an instructor in the Ambulance Service, I had to set objectives not only for my students, but for myself. One day, during my Instructional Methods training course, I was struggling to come up with a lesson plan. My trainer tried to help me by asking, 'If you don't know where you're going, how are you going to get there?' It was sound advice and I went on to pass my course.

But in my present situation, I didn't have an answer to either the 'where' or the 'how'. I was going to have to make it up as I went.

I wrote *Bright Lights and Fairy Dust* by typing up the journal I kept as Linda's cancer progressed.

After she died, I carried on writing, but this time about me. As I had written in the journal every day, maybe I had to ease myself away from the pen and paper in order that I wouldn't suffer withdrawal. I might have even tricked myself into thinking I still had Linda. To care for, to make notes for, to touch and to kiss. Perhaps, by writing, I could keep her with me; she hadn't died at all. So I wrote *to* Linda and *about* Linda and when I experienced anything that brought to mind a strong memory or emotion, I jotted down my thoughts.

The notes, letters, emails and conversations that follow are a record of literary and vocal exchanges, all of which have helped me to move forward, if only in some small way. And although I have put them down in chronological order, I have made a point of leaving out specific dates, using asterisks instead to punctuate blocks of time.

One

Five Minutes

S he's gone.

These were the two words I spoke at the very moment you left us and I know they are strange to hear when I say them out loud again now. They're also strange to look at on the page. But, as I think back, they absolutely described your passing. You were gone from us to another place. We weren't able to go with you and we are left here, separated from you physically.

Wayne, Sara and I leaned across your bed and hugged you, and one another, like forwards in a rugby scrum. Then we sat back, in some form of shock I think. Even though we always knew it would happen, when you took your last breath we almost could not believe what we had witnessed.

I could not cry, not then. Perhaps it was my training, so deep in my psyche that I went into action without even realising. I had the need to be strong. There would be a lot to do and I had to keep a clear head. I called the doctor back to the house one last time. I wanted him to attend; to hear it from him.

Dr. Sandhu's presence was reassuring. I never left you for a moment, but it was for the doctor to disconnect the syringe driver and to remove your cannula and catheter, which he did with care and consideration. It made me feel as though he was setting you free at last. Free from the dreadful illness; from the paraphernalia of treatment. Free from pain.

The undertakers were also very gentle and caring. Theirs cannot be a pleasant job at the best of times – although I don't suppose there are many of those – and moving you wasn't without its problems. The cancer had broken out of you. I remember one of the District Nurses saying that in all her years of nursing she had never seen anyone carry a tumour for so long. In her experience, cancer such as yours had claimed the patient's life long before it came to the surface. It was another measure of how strong you were.

Although I didn't have to, I helped the undertakers to transfer you from the bed (which I'd lowered) onto the sheet and into the body bag. As well as lifting it, they had to raise the framed bag in order to get you round the corner and into the hallway. Dolly, you were almost standing upright! I followed them out of the house. I wanted to be sure that the move went as well as it could and I wanted to know with certainty that you left your house with all the dignity you deserved, despite the mild comedy that preceded your departure.

Then I watched them take you away.

Five Hours

I couldn't sleep much, so I got up early.

Today – Monday – wasn't just another day, it was the first day of the rest of my life without you. Even as I woke, my mind was racing and my body buzzing with an overload of synapses, hormones and chemicals, all of which fuelled me to keep going in an automatic way. It was just as well, because I knew there would be a great deal to do, especially as it was now a weekday and the people I needed to contact would be available, at work. Although I might have appeared cool, collected and in control, I felt as if I might burst with the strain of my emotions.

I first spoke to your GP who said she would leave the 'certificate of death' at the surgery reception by lunchtime. This wasn't the Death Certificate – I would have to get that from the Registrar – but I needed the doctor's certificate of death in order to get the Death Certificate. What your GP was completing was a 'Medical Certificate of Cause of Death' and it was my duty, as 'the informant', to take this to the Registrar as soon as possible or within five days.

Through a family contact, I was able to arrange for the medical equipment that had been loaned by the NHS to be collected today. You knew – and I had heard – that it could sometimes take weeks to have stuff picked up, so this was a massive load off my mind. Last night, Wayne and I dismantled the hospital bed and took almost all of the equipment out of the dining room and placed it in the garage, swapping it for the table and chairs that had been stored there. At first, I felt it was very cold of me to have reinstated the dining room so soon after your death, but I tempered my unease by reasoning that it certainly couldn't stay as it was.

With the furniture back in the room, it was almost as though nothing had happened. The evidence had been removed and the house was no longer the nursing environment it had been just hours earlier. However, to this day a permanent reminder remains in the form of two deep track marks in the wooden floor of the lounge and dining room. These were caused by the castors on that massive recliner chair you borrowed, which I dragged across the floor on my own after you had become bed-bound. I wanted to be next to you. If I'd known it was going to do that I would have asked someone to help me. I can only see it in certain light when I look across from the kitchen. Some visitors probably haven't even noticed it.

I contacted the funeral directors and arranged for Wayne, Sara and me to meet them at 11.00 a.m. Then I gathered together all the clothing and accessories that you had told me ages ago that you wanted to be buried in. I put your lime green wedding outfit, lime green square-cut tee shirt, brown beads and brown pointy shoes in a bag. I also put one of your wigs in. You lost your own hair when you had radiotherapy, after which it only grew back a little. You still liked to wear the wig occasionally.

A panic set in when I couldn't find your wedding and engagement rings. I knew you wanted to wear them, but you'd taken them off a long time ago when your fingers had swollen up. I didn't know where you'd put them. Wayne, Sara and I began to look in all the obvious places: drawers, dresser and jewellery box, all to no avail. Then Wayne called out that he had found them. They were in one of your little papier mâché trinket boxes on the mantel shelf, a little heart-shaped one painted in blue and cream. He couldn't say what had drawn him to it and I didn't recall you placing your rings in it, so we thought you might have lent a helping hand in the search.

I also contacted the Register Office and made an afternoon appointment to register your death. It all seemed so unreal, and yet the harsh reality had to be faced: you had died; you had moved into another plane; gone over to the other side. It didn't matter which way I looked at it, it all came down to the same thing. You, my Darling Linda, were gone from me and from us. What would I do now? How would I ever cope? Remember the words of the song I wrote for you: *You are my life, You are my every day*? I felt that I had no more life, no more days. As tough as I was finding it all, I knew I had to snap out of this if I was ever going to be able to function at this intense, yet important time.

Once everything had been set up, Wayne, Sara and I walked into town. We went to the funeral directors first, where we were met by one of the staff and taken through to the lounge for an informal chat. We looked at coffin brochures – a first for me – and although the situation seemed unbelievable at the time, the three of us agreed on one that we thought you would like. I passed across the bag of your things that I had put together and was told that they would dress you and that we could come back later to see you in your finery. We still had other errands to run so we arranged to return at 3.30 p.m. when I would place your rings back on your wedding finger just I had done when we first fell in love and then married.

The funeral directors discussed possible funeral dates. Acorn Ridge, the woodland burial site that you had decided on a few months earlier, only like to do one funeral a day and they were booked out on Thursday and Friday that week, which would put us into next week. On checking with the church, the funeral directors were told that St. John's was unavailable all of next week. This meant your funeral would have to be the week after, which, by coincidence, was the week of our wedding anniversary. But if that was the first available date then we would take it.

It was a fine and dry autumn day and our walk to the Register Office was pleasant enough in the circumstances. The process of registering your death was also straight forward. I handed the registrar the letter the doctor had left for me. In return, I received the Green Form – granting permission for your burial – which I would need to pass to the funeral directors, and a copy of the Death Certificate. In fact, I asked for ten copies, thinking I would need that many to send off to various authorities.

Without needing to rush to make it in time for our appointment, we returned to the funeral directors and after another brief talk with the staff, were shown along the corridor to the Chapel of Rest.

We saw that you were dressed exactly as you had wanted to be. Wayne and Sara went to your right, I to your left to put your engagement and wedding rings on. I couldn't help noticing that clear fluid had leaked slightly into your clothes on my side. I knew what it was but I was surprised at how quickly it had happened, bearing in mind that you had probably only been wearing the change of clothes for a couple of hours. I said nothing, but I wished I hadn't seen it because it left me feeling upset and uneasy.

We left you with a kiss goodbye and spoke once more with the staff. They had been in touch again with both the church and the woodland burial site and suddenly it could all be done in three days time. We had some work to do now, getting the message out to everyone.

As we were leaving, I passed another item of yours to the staff and asked them to put it on top of your coffin. It was a black bandana. A very special black bandana.

*****

Back in August, we received an e-mail from our friends in Australia:

> *Thursday 2355hrs*
> *From: John and Leonie*
> *To: Chris and Linda*
> *Subject: Hi*

Hi Chris & Linda,

Just a quick message to see how you are going and to let you know that we think of you often. It has been a while since you last spoke to Mum, so I thought that I would let you know that you are both in all our thoughts.
We are working away as usual and the year is absolutely flying by. We have no news really.
I won't waffle on. Just wanted to say 'Hi'.

Love
Leonie

With everything that was going on at the time, I never got round to replying then, but now I did:

Tuesday 1047hrs
From: Chris
To: John and Leonie
Subject: Linda

Dear John and Leonie

Thank you for your most recent e-mail and kind words. I am sorry for the delay in responding.

I'm writing to let you know that Linda died on Sunday, at tea time.

The last twenty-four hours of her life were difficult, as she fought not only the disease, but the medication too. She never once gave up

fighting. Eventually, though, her racked body could take no more and she died peacefully at home with Wayne, Sara and me holding her. The room was filled with love, choral music was playing gently in the background, the sun was shining and her bed faced the garden.
Linda's wishes regarding dying were totally fulfilled. What an achievement in death.

We (Wayne, Sara and I) have been on the receiving end of some strange magic. For example, choosing her burial place this time last week was like it was meant to be. And yesterday, I panicked when I couldn't find her wedding or engagement rings. Wayne walked into the lounge and, without knowing why, he went straight to a little heart-shaped box on the mantle shelf. The rings were inside it. It meant we could take them to the Chapel of Rest so that I could place them on Linda's finger. Then, this morning, we have been working on the order of service. I couldn't find a suitable photo for it. Breaking off from that project, I went to the pin board in our pantry, to try to find a number for the local hospital. In one corner there was a torn piece of paper with Linda's picture on it, from a sheet Linda and I had done for someone a couple of years ago. 'That's the picture we should use', Sara said.
The most incredible bit of magic, though, happened to my Mum yesterday morning. She went out to her car and a white feather had drifted on to the window, just above the driver's

door lock, and got wedged in the rubber. My Mum won't touch it. She'll let it come off on its own. Linda always told Mum she was getting her wings.
I can't explain these events, so I love the idea that the fairies are looking after us.

We are holding Linda's funeral this Thursday, at 2.00 p.m.
I'll let you know how it goes and will try to write again soon.

Linda composed a poem for me just hours before she was unable to string any more words together. I wrote it down:
'Diddly di; Diddly do; Chris, I'm so in love with you'
I miss my Darling wife so very much but, as painful and as heavy as my heart is now, I would not have wished her any further pain. The end had come and we knew it. She knew it, too.

Lots of love to you all and thank you, everyone, for your love and support. It has helped us all so much and continues to do so.

Chris
xxx

It was important that we did not delay in sending out word of your death. Using the technology with which he is most familiar, Wayne went up to the study and set to work on your side of the family – the Marshall side.

For my part, I went through the address book that I got from the kitchen shelf – the book that you maintained better than I ever did. With a pencil, I drew a large tick through those names I could contact.

'The London Army is mobilising,' Wayne said when he came downstairs.

*****

There was plenty to do. I still hadn't slept well all week and I knew I was becoming exhausted, but I had to keep going. Wayne and I went out to copy the Order of Service. The self-service copier wouldn't do what I wanted, which was to copy two-sided to two-sided, so the man in the print area said that he would do it for me at the same price. He told us to go for a coffee, as it would take about twenty minutes.

We went across to Burger King and sat down with a large Americano each. Lowering my defences, and slightly brushing aside my training, I confessed to Wayne that I wasn't having a very good day. Neither was he. Just as I did not know the pain of a parent dying, so it was impossible for Wayne to know the pain felt by a widower.

In the afternoon I went to the church, to take all of the fifty or so extra chairs from the parish room and put them out in the main church. There were 150 permanent seats, but I had a feeling we would need more than that. And with the Musical Director, I also ran through the music we had put on to a disc for your service. He set up a CD player upstairs in the choir and I went to the front of the church and faced the sanctuary. Both of us checked the volume as the music tumbled into the nave. I tried to imagine what it would be like the next day, but I couldn't. This was the church where you and I were blessed after getting married; where Wayne was confirmed; where my parents had renewed their vows after fifty years of marriage; where you and I had only recently renewed our wedding vows. I could only recall the joyful services there and it seemed too far-fetched to think that it was your funeral that was going to be taking place there the next day.

I had worked on some short text for the announcement in the local paper. Sorry, Darling, this was simply a bulletin. I haven't had time for a full obituary, but I will aim to do that next week. I just hope I'm not too late to get this into print in tomorrow's paper.

Wednesday 1535hrs
From: Chris Page.
To: Molly French, Funeral Directors
Subject: Newspaper entry for the late Linda Page

Dear Molly,

Sorry for the delay. Please see below some text for this week's paper.

PAGE. Linda. On Sunday Linda died peacefully at home, surrounded by family and friends.
The funeral service will take place at 2.00pm on Thursday, at St. John's Church, Newbury. All welcome.

Family flowers only, but donations may be made to the Berkshire Cancer Centre Fund.

Thank you.
Regards
Chris

Look at that subject heading and see how quickly I have used the term *late*. It's only been three days and already my dictionary has expanded to include many of the terms reserved for families in our situation. As much as it upsets me, I'm sure it's the right word. Something else for me to grapple with.

I received an e-mail reply from Australia this evening.

Wednesday 1920hrs
From: John and Leonie
To: Chris
Subject: Linda

What a terrible ordeal you have lived through
this last year. I can't imagine what you must
have been through. It seems though, now that
Linda has gone, you have managed to find some
sort of peaceful resolution from within.
The way you described her passing is so
beautiful. At home, in the place she loves, with
the people she loves. It is so wonderful that
Linda's last hours and moments were spent like
this. No wonder she left a little bit of magic
behind.

*You say she is getting her wings. Mum said to
me just yesterday that she is getting her butterfly
wings. Look out for any beautiful butterflies
fluttering around your garden. They could have
a connection to your beautiful Linda.
Only the body dies Chris. The spirit lives on, the
soul lives on and the love lives on and, of
course, the magic lives on.
I know your heart must be so heavy right now,
but isn't it wonderful that you had Linda in your
life and that you shared so much together?
Lots of love to you Chris and we will all be
thinking of you over the next few days as you lay
Linda in her final resting place.*

Leonie
x

*****

It's the day of your funeral and burial.

Wayne, Sara and I had worked flat out to arrange everything in the short time we had. Among us we managed to contact almost everyone in the family and also in our address book. Those we couldn't get hold of would be informed subsequently.

We had chosen the coffin and made arrangements with the funeral directors regarding the hearse and cars. Details of the service were put in the paper, but only just in time for today's print run. I'm sorry, Darling, I would have preferred to have given people more notice, but it couldn't be helped.

Father Bernard had recently retired, so it was Father Trevor who had come to the house and helped us to form an Order of Service. I didn't know what hymns to use, but I told him I definitely didn't want *Abide With Me*. 'Oh, thank God for that!' he exclaimed. This made us all laugh and Father Trevor had thus put us at ease, suggesting more appropriate hymns together with prayers and readings. We wanted to include some music of our own choosing. My sister Linda has written a poem. Your sister Jenni has written a sonnet, based on the sonnets of Michelangelo.

We had agreed that the cortege should leave from the house and that we would have one limousine for the three of us and Mum and Dad. At the appointed time the hearse arrived in the street and I went straight out to greet it – to see you. There were flowers on and around your beautiful wicker coffin. Stitched to the wickerwork on the top there was a red rose and the black bandana, the 'Wagamama' bandana I had asked the funeral directors to place on the top. It was neatly folded, almost flag-like, to show off the word to best effect. With bold white lettering and a red star above the first 'm', this was restaurant apparel, which Wayne had managed to pick up for you from somewhere in the world. He's Wag. You're Wagamama. It was perfect.

'Good job,' I said to Pelham, the man in charge; the man with the top hat. I only just managed to get the words out, for I was so full of emotion that I thought I would break at any moment. I returned briefly to the house and we gathered ourselves for the journey to the church.

'We'll be strong,' I said. 'We'll be strong for Linda. We can do this.'

Pelham walked ahead of the hearse and our limousine, holding back the traffic just as we wanted him to. We reckoned that would get your thumbs up. He walked for a couple of hundred yards before getting back into the hearse for the last leg of the first part of the journey, which was to the church and which wasn't far.

When the funeral cars pulled into the car park there were very few people around. Pelham went into the church, I guessed to assess the situation.

'It's absolutely full,' he said when he came out. 'Standing room only.'

We had also agreed that I would be the first in line behind the coffin, walking alone. Wayne and Sara would follow, then Mum and Dad. I focussed my entire being on the job to be done. I didn't want to be seen to falter in front of a church full of people. As we all went in, I was aware that the church was indeed full – to overflowing actually – but I dared not look at anyone. Your wicker coffin creaked as it was placed on a trolley. I fixed my gaze on the brass name plate on top, placed my fingertips on the edge of the wickerwork and followed you in, as attached to you as I could possibly be. At the front of the church five chairs had been reserved for us and I took my place there. Physically I could not have been any closer to you at that moment in time; emotionally I was, and I am, tied to you.

A prayer was said:

> *Father, the death of Linda brings an emptiness into our lives. We are separated from her and we feel broken and disturbed. Give us confidence that she is safe and her life complete with you, and bring us together at the last to the wholeness and fullness of your presence in heaven, where*

*your saints and your angels enjoy you forever
and ever, amen.*

The hymn, *Praise My Soul The King Of Heaven*
followed, and then a reading from John's Gospel. I had
arranged with the church to play a CD track. It was
from one of your favourite albums, *Cherish The Ladies*.
I struggled to hold myself together as the congregation
listened to *I'll Walk Beside You* and I felt as though it
could have been written just for this moment.

My sister Linda read out her poem; Jenni her sonnet.
Two more hymns were sung and further prayers were
offered, including, in recognition of your catholic
upbringing, the Hail Mary. The church service concluded
with another CD track. You loved *Coldplay*. Wayne,
Sara and I had chosen *Yellow* for you. It had been played
at your nephew David's funeral.

I may never listen to it again.

After the service, we went to Acorn Ridge, to the
place you had chosen – that *we* had chosen. I recalled
the day I had gone there to pick the exact spot. You
were too ill to come with me that day and it was left to
me to decide on one of two plots we were offered, each
marked with a white plastic stake. As it turned out, the
one I selected was where you had your photo taken
with Wayne three weeks earlier at the beginning of
September.

Now, I was back. The white stake was gone and
your grave had been dug, but, if only for a moment, I
was taken aback. It was huge. The hole wasn't just
deep, it was wide. It had to be nearly four feet across,
almost the size of a double bed. Your wicker coffin was

certainly wider than a wooden one, but I couldn't help wondering what dimensions the funeral directors had given Acorn Ridge.

Many of those who had attended the church were able to come to your burial service. Words and prayers were offered for you and for us who mourn you. I looked down to where you now lay. Only the Wagamama bandana and my single red rose remained in place on the wicker background. The one-word sentiment that I had written on the florist's tag was just visible.

'Forever'.

From Acorn Ridge, we repaired to our local for your wake. Oh dear me, what shocking vocabulary that is. Along with *cancer, terminal, dying, death, late, gone, undertakers, funeral* and *grave, wake* is on the growing list of woeful words that I now seem to be using regularly.

I remember when you asked Veronique if you could have your wake here. She was a little shocked at your bold request, but you knew what you wanted and she was pleased to be able to do this for you.

Although at first it felt wrong to think of your wake as a reception or a party, in my view it was both these things. It was a celebration of you and your life. Guests talked about you; remembered you.

For me, for you, and, perhaps, for many others too, it was important that we did this, as painful as it was.

It went well, Darling. Sorry, it sounds awful to say it like that, but as celebrations go it was a success. Lots of people were there. I fear I may not have spoken to them all, even though I tried to circulate. I do know that there was plenty of conversation among family and friends. Veronique's spread looked great, but was always just out of my reach as I went round talking to people. It was late when it eventually wrapped up.

When I got home I started making notes in advance of my appointment with the Clinical Psychologist the next day. The appointment was in fact yours – (ours, because I would have gone with you) – but I saw no reason to skip it. On the contrary, I wanted to keep it because I had so many questions and thoughts racing around in my head that I wondered if the psychologist could help me sort them out.

Here's a list I made of the feelings I am aware of and my scribbles for the appointment. I just threw them down on to the page in my journal, so I apologise if they look a little erratic.

- *Desolation*
- *Emptiness*
- *Anger*
- *Sadness – that Linda slowly lost everything*
- *Guilt – for ever getting angry with Linda and her illness*
- *Disbelief – is this real?*
- *I know no one could have done more for Linda. She had such fantastic support around her, from family and friends and from healthcare professionals.*
- *Reflecting back now, on our 'journey', I knew Linda was going to die, so I knew where we were going. I didn't know how we'd get there,*

or when. On the day it happened, the journey didn't matter anymore; we had arrived. And yet it DOES matter.

- *In cushioning my Son, have I displaced myself as regards the grieving process?*
- *I feel such deep sorrow for Linda, with her physical changes throughout the disease, and feel continuing sorrow in this regard, having seen her in the Chapel of Rest.*
- *In the same way, when we were journeying, I couldn't imagine how I would cope without her. I feel I'm on another journey now and can't imagine how I'll be in a week, a month, a year. (DON'T TRY TO IMAGINE!)*
- *I'd like my grief to be my own, but I feel I may be grieving for Linda <u>and</u> Wayne. But I want the opposite for him. I want him to grieve for himself and leave me to grieve. I'm all mixed up.*
- *Only last week, Linda was eating (and eating well). The disbelief that she's actually gone.*
- *I get frequent flashbacks to the Chapel of Rest, to the fluid on Linda's clothes. I would like to get some happier images and memories back into my head.*
- *I keep having a bad dream about the leaking fluid. I have to fold her clothing and wrap it round the fluid then wait for somebody. It doesn't seem to be about closure.*
- *I have felt that I had to be strong for my Son and I wonder if that was, after all, the right way. Is there a 'right way'?*
- *Linda's cancer was so cruel. Brenda and David didn't suffer the incapacity that befell Linda.*

Five Days

I had run myself right down over the course of the final weeks and days of your illness. You knew that.

I heard you telling the District Nurse one day, while I was loading the washing machine. She was attending to you in your bed by the patio doors.

'He never stops,' you said. 'I worry about him.'

And then you called me to get away from that particular duty.

'Come on, Chris. Come and sit down. Leave that.'

But I couldn't and I didn't. I was keeping house as best I could. Never as good as you had done, but we had standards to maintain and anyway I wanted to do it. I didn't want a cleaner, or a housekeeper. I didn't want someone else cooking for us and I certainly didn't want anyone poking around in our kitchen. Giving in to that would have been admitting defeat and neither of us was going to do that if we could help it.

By bedtime I was exhausted from our day's activities, yet I would not have changed a thing and I have no regrets. You were always my main concern. However, you will remember how snappy I had become. I was short on sleep, short on temper and, after a long day, I had a face to match. I don't think I had taken much notice Darling, but I had begun to lose weight. My face had become skinny and drawn; my hair even paler than the grey we had come to accept. Even as I tried to take care of myself, I know I had not done so properly for several days. The strain of knowing that we were soon going to have to say goodbye was showing on me. I shall forever remain sorry that I snapped at you as you struggled through pain and that long, long night just days before you left us.

*****

I kept our appointment with the Clinical Psychologist. She did a lot of listening as I went through my list. I felt I was allowed to air my feelings, but I didn't receive any advice and I'm not sure if I was disappointed by or approving of this. Who can guide me through my grief?

There is no script, the Psychologist advised me. There's no time frame and no order to the things I would be feeling.

*****

Wayne and Sara left the East Fields to go back to their home in London. I was left to my thoughts and memories. I logged in to my desktop computer and began typing your obituary to put in the local paper. In my head, I had been working on it for a couple of days and it was time now to empty my thoughts into the keyboard.

During the course of the day, the phone rang with far more regularity than I thought I wanted, but every call helped me to take another little step forward. Pat and Dinah invited me to their house for some lunch and

I walked there at 1.20 p.m. I let them read a rough draft of what I'd worked on during the morning. The gist of what I wanted to say was there, but it needed to be improved.

When I got home, I went up to the crow's nest for a light snooze, because tiredness of great proportion had overcome me. I lay on the bed. Half propped up with lots of pillows, I felt myself starting to nod off. Then I thought I had died for a split second as I went off to sleep. I felt my breathing had stopped and then restarted, just like you with your sleep apnoea.

There were more phone calls during the afternoon and I carried on working on your obituary. I called Wayne and ran it past him. After talking it through, I made some further changes and worked late into the evening. It was 11.30 p.m. when I finally went to bed. I still had that little tickle on my chest, but I thought it wasn't as bad. 'Stress asthma' I call it.

It was my first night alone in the house.

*****

Once again I had an unsettled night, waking up frequently throughout. There was a silence I hadn't noticed before: no one sleeping in the next room, or in the crow's nest. It was just me, wriggling and squirming in our big, brass bed and wrestling with thoughts and memories. I couldn't get that tune out of my head, the one that played as we left the church to go to Acorn Ridge; the one that makes me so sad. *Yellow*. I kept going over the whole thing: your illness, your death, your funeral and burial. As I lay there in bed, I was still in disbelief that you are gone forever and I wondered how I would ever move forward.

Eventually I got up and started going through more documentation and made copies of the Nursing Care Plan, because I knew the District Nurse would be taking the originals away the next day and I wanted a record kept here for you. For me. I still couldn't let go.

I made a pathetic start on clearing the drug drawers, which were full of your medication, and I broke down as I dried your *Linda* mug and went to put it away.

'Oh, Baby, Baby,' I wailed aloud, 'I love you so much. I promise I'm trying to be strong.'

In the afternoon, I drove to Penton for Emma's Christening. In April you had held Emma – David and Nicola's new baby – in your arms, and we were invited to her Christening. In your absence I pledged I would still go, although I felt sad and alone. As I drove into Hampshire I howled and screamed in the car, much more loudly than I could ever have done at home without attracting attention to myself. But in the car I might as well have been in outer space: no one could hear me scream.

The service was sweet and the congregation sang *All Things Bright And Beautiful* completely a cappella. I don't know if it was intentional or because there wasn't an organist (or possibly even an organ) but I'd never sung like that before in a church.

I couldn't stay for long at the party afterwards. Even though it was very well attended I pined for you. I was surrounded by people and yet I felt as though I was on my own. After a cup of tea I apologised that I was taking my leave and drove home, howling loudly, almost wolf-like, for much of the way.

In the evening, as I looked at photographs of you, I found myself getting rushes of adrenaline, anxiety and anger, and even clearing your make up bags upset me to tears. The phone rang some more and I described my feelings of desolation, emptiness, anger and disbelief to two more caring friends who had called to support me.

I miss you, Darling. Will I ever feel okay again?

In the few days we had to arrange your funeral I had tried unsuccessfully to get hold of some dear friends with whom you had regularly exchanged correspondence for over twenty five years. It was important to me that they should know, so I sat down and wrote a card to them:

> *Please forgive that I have resorted to writing to you, but the only number I have for you is a mobile one and it has been switched off each time I've rung this week.*
>
> *I need you to know that my Darling Linda died on Sunday. She died here at home, with me, Wayne and Sara holding her gently. It was always the case that the wretched cancer would consume her and in the last week of her life the cancer seemed to double and double very quickly. Her poor body was racked with a pain that neither she, nor any of us here, could bear anymore. Linda elected to go on the syringe driver Saturday lunchtime. That evening she lost the ability to string words together and couldn't take oral medication. On Sunday, I had to call the out-of-hours doctor. I called him twice more as Linda continued to deteriorate. Ultimately I called him to confirm death.*

My heart is so heavy I cannot begin to explain the pain I feel. Linda was my world.
I will love Linda all my life; and Wayne, too. He is also hurting badly, but with Sara there with us we will, all three, move forward.
I'm so sorry that this sad news had to come to you in a letter.
My kind regards to you both,
Chris

Perhaps not surprisingly I had another bad night. I slept only from midnight until about three then remained unsettled. I tried to read, but gave up trying to share my concentration with the printed word and got up at 6.30 a.m. Fleeting thoughts of regret entered my head, that I couldn't or didn't go with you on your journey. Surely, I couldn't be the only bereaved person to think along those lines?

There were more phone calls. I contacted Air Liquide to cancel the oxygen and report the final reading. I phoned one of the Macmillan nurses to ask if I could meet with the Palliative Care Consultant on Wednesday. I hoped he might be able to help settle my mind. I wanted to ask him, for example, if yours had been a peaceful death, because I didn't think so. I wanted to tell him about the dream I keep having, about the body fluids I'd witnessed in the Chapel of Rest. The Macmillan nurse told me I was trying to run before I could walk.

'Don't think about any more than an hour at a time,' she said. 'You're probably thinking you wish you could have gone with her.'

How did she know that?

'I've just got to get it into my head,' I said, 'that she's not coming back.'

'Whoah!' she replied. 'You're trying to move too fast. She's only just died.' She tried to comfort me. 'What you did for Linda was so intense that now she's gone you probably feel you've got too much time on your hands. There's lots to do, don't get me wrong, but you're not having to care for Linda. Remember, Chris, no one ever died of a broken heart.'

I thought I would.

The Macmillan nurse said she would ask The Palliative Care Consultant to call me, which he did that afternoon. I told him everything I'd told her and added that I continued to feel a deep regret that because I'd been dissuaded from doing so, I hadn't been to see you again in the Chapel. He suggested that it might help me to speak to the person who had prepared you for the Chapel, so when our call ended I arranged to do that.

I visited our neighbours. I told them how difficult I was finding things, but that I was doing my best to stay strong.

'My Linda went from me on the Saturday night, when she couldn't take the tablets or put a sentence together.'

I think that as well as telling them, I was also actually telling myself out loud what I thought might help *me*.

When I got home I continued to work through the drug drawers, snapping pills out of blister packs and putting them into a large, clear plastic bag. I planned to take them back to the pharmacy for disposal in a single bag. There were pills that had worked, pills that might have worked; pills that you tried, pills that made you better and made you worse, morphine tablets, antibiotics and so on. I was late to bed again.

I held on to the liquid morphine. I thought I might make use of it.

I currently have some health issues. My mouth is full of ulcers, my tongue is black and I have what I am calling 'stress asthma'. My right ear is uncomfortable, painful even. We know our own bodies. You knew something was wrong when you had that lump. I know this ear problem is real, even though both the practice nurse and the doctor have said there's nothing there. And my tongue, my black tongue. I looked it up on the internet. It's sometimes called brown tongue, but mine is definitely black. The internet article informed me that the condition is also called glossophytis and is caused by a type of black fungus which can grow on the tongue under certain conditions. In many instances the cause is not known, but it can be the result of taking antibiotics (not so, in my case), inappropriate diet (sounds like me), or poor oral hygiene (I try to look after my mouth). *'It may also be associated with stress and a depressive illness',* the article read. Aha! I might actually fit the patient profile after all. Anyone can get it, especially the elderly, the frail and the infirm. Whoa! Hold on. Let's stick with stress, can we? What about treatment? The article suggested a pineapple cure. I am to slice a whole pineapple and then use one slice for each treatment. The slice must be cut further, into eight segments, and each segment is to be placed on my tongue for thirty to forty seconds. I am to spit out the segment and do the same with each one until the entire slice has been used up. This is to be done twice a day for between seven and ten days. I didn't know, until I found this out on the computer, that pineapple contains *salicylic acid*. This is the basis of aspirin and perhaps this is why the laying on of pineapple on one's tongue is supposed to work a cure. Anyway, I'm going to try it. I would like here to credit the article to its author, Professor John Murtagh of Australia.

In the meantime, along with my awful tongue and dull ear ache, I seem also to be struggling with appetite, weight loss and bowel motility. I suppose all this has come about because I didn't take care of myself while I was caring for you. It's my own fault; I should have realised sooner. I must have been living on hormones, my endocrine system pushing out clever chemicals like adrenaline and thyroid T3 and T4, or else it was stress and responsibility that kept me going when really my body was crying out for its own respite.

I should be able now to start fixing these things, but I still don't sleep properly. Nor am I eating properly. I'm trying hard to cook proper meals, but cooking for one is not coming easily. I find myself cooking for you and me, as usual, so your helping goes into a plastic container and either I freeze it or else save it for the next day. Even buying food for one is difficult. Am I ever going to function without you, Dolly?

*****

I was disappointed, when I woke, to see the clock displaying 2.20 a.m. On and off, for the rest of the night, I tried to tune in to my somnolence, but I didn't manage proper sleep. I got up at 7.30 a.m. I don't know why, but I had the tune from *Hill Street Blues* in my head and images of a dark pick-up truck arriving home and a chap in a checked shirt getting out of it. I couldn't make sense of that.

Pat phoned. He tried to encourage me back to the music; to the band. I couldn't imagine myself playing and singing again. I had been away from it for so long that for one thing I wasn't sure I'd remember how to play. And the thought of going public as a performing widower didn't exactly inspire me either. The combination had me recoiling from his suggestion and I think I wanted to run away from it.

A man with a van arrived at nine, to collect the riser/recliner chair – the chair that had done Wayne's back in when he and I had carried it from the dining room into the garage; the chair that had carved its tracks in our dining room floor. I gave him a hand, but it still took some effort to heave it up into the van.

I arranged to go to the funeral directors and went there in the morning to hand over another contribution to the Berkshire Cancer Centre fund that we'd organised after your passing. My main reason for going, though, was to talk to the lady who had dressed you. I hoped she could put my mind at ease about what had gone on.

She was very supportive and explained that it was merely interstitial fluid[1] that had come from your cancer and your leg, but it had become a problem

---

[1] Interstitial fluid is the fluid that surrounds body tissue cells and in which our body cells are bathed. It contains around one quarter of the water in the human body. And a human body contains something like 50 to 65 percent water.

because no matter how much they padded it, it still leaked. They had felt it best for the family to remember you as you were and they thanked me for discouraging some family members from visiting the Chapel of Rest. She said my experience and understanding had made things easier for them.

'You've got nothing to be cross with yourself about, Mr. Page. You got the rings on and that was great. And you saw the fluid. It was just fluid. It was only that it was soaking into her clothes. She looked the same as she did on Monday. It's best that the family remembers her as she was before.'

'And the funeral?' I asked her. 'Was that brought forward because of the fluid problem?'

'No, it's just how it worked out. With Acorn Ridge, with a natural burial, especially when there's cancer, the sooner the burial the better. We could have embalmed Linda and that would have stopped the leaking and made things much tidier, but we didn't need to.'

I recalled the terms and conditions of the woodland burial site.

'But they wouldn't have taken her if she'd been embalmed,' I replied.

'Exactly. So it all worked out in the end. Even Pelham said, when he got back, 'That went off well'. You're talked about every day.'

I handed over the large sum of money that by now had come to me at home in cards of condolence, and the lady totted up the amount so far raised. It was a considerable amount already and donations were still coming in, she told me.

*****

The next morning I was up at six and I'd shaved, showered and had left home by 7.20 a.m. to go the hospital. I returned the chair-raising 'elephant feet' and took your other wig – your first wig, I mean – to the Day Therapy Unit. I thought someone else might be able to make use of it.

The Palliative Care Consultant made the tea. My meeting with him lasted a whole hour, but afterwards I felt that he had helped me to allay some of the issues that concerned me. I stayed on at the unit, chatting to the staff and friends that you and I had come to know over the months that we went there. I even had lunch with them, just as you and I used to.

*****

Another early start and although I got up early, I had managed four hours sleep. I was out of the house by 7.30 a.m. because I wanted to go to the supermarket. I had to know whether or not your obituary had gone into the local paper.

It had.

There were some very minor changes to what I'd written but none that I needed to complain about.

I also returned the pyjamas and a tee shirt that you'd bought there only a few weeks earlier but didn't get around to wearing.

I spent the afternoon sorting out more documents and went for a 1.00 p.m. appointment at the bank. Our joint accounts and mortgage now had to reflect the change in our circumstances. Aldo was the very understanding and sympathetic man who conducted our meeting. A new cheque book will be sent to me.

Your name will be missing. The mortgage, however, will take a little longer to sort out.

Oh, Darling, this is all so painful.

After my meeting, I went to Acorn Ridge with Mum and Dad. I wanted to have a look at the stone tablets on other plots, to give me an idea of what was possible. Based on what I saw I reckoned we could have 'Wagamama' engraved and I sketched out a couple of ideas on a sheet of A4 paper.

*****

Sleep is lasting longer and the bad dreams or images haven't come for two nights in a row. I woke at five this morning, but waking up alone is sad. It's sad that you're not there, that you're not doing that breathing thing you used to do. Oh, Linda, I miss you.

I found it difficult to continue going through the paperwork this morning, so instead I sorted out flowers, did the washing up, put some washing on and tumble dried it afterwards. I called the practice nurse at the surgery about my self-diagnosed 'stress asthma' and she asked if I could pop in. I couldn't, as I had more errands to run, but when I got back she had popped a prescription through the door for an inhaler.

During the evening I made a start on a picture project. I want to gather together lots of photographs of what we did together after your diagnosis. To fit them all in a frame I've decided to make them small. There are lots of photos on the computer, so this is going to take a while to sort out.

*****

What a dreadful night. I'd fallen asleep quickly, but woke half an hour after midnight. I managed to get back to sleep but then woke again at 4.30 a.m. and thrashed around until 6.00 a.m. It was just getting light and a half moon was high in the sky. I wondered how it had fared, after the rocket crashes yesterday, and I hoped it was okay.

You probably wonder what I mean, but the day before, you see, NASA had crashed two unmanned spacecraft into the moon, to look for evidence of water. The first crashed into the moon's south pole at lunchtime our time and was expected to send up debris from the resulting crater, which would be analysed for any signs of water by the second spacecraft on its way down to the surface. The mission was called LCROSS (the Lunar Crater Observation and Sensing Satellite).

Scientists were disappointed though. There was no debris.

My loneliness was no more healed than yesterday or the day before and I kept reminding myself that the whole grieving process was going to take a very long time and, as the psychologist had told me, there was no script.

Pat, Dinah, Ken and I went to Lacock in Wiltshire today. It was the trip you and I cancelled when your pathological fracture[2] was diagnosed and I think we all

---

[2] A Pathological Bone Fracture is one resulting from a disease that has caused weakness in the bone, where little or no external trauma is involved. The most common cause is osteoporosis, but it can also be due to cancer, infection, inherited bone disorder or a cyst on the bone.

felt we owed it to you to go there. In a strange kind of way we took you with us, because it was in your memory that we went. But I realised when we visited the abbey that it wasn't suitable for wheelchairs. I remembered how you fretted about the sixteen steps that Pat had told us there were, because you didn't want to be hauled around like a piece of cargo.

You were right, Dolly.

We enjoyed our day out in the pretty village though, taking in the old buildings; the abbey; the history. After a fine lunch in the busy Carpenter's Arms, I lit a candle for you in St. Cyriac's church just along the road.

I slept well that night. I woke at five but drifted off again until six before getting up. I felt as though I had to force myself to do anything, so I forced myself to shave, to shower, to floss. The feeling in the back of my throat was still uncomfortable. It wasn't sore, like the sore throat I get when I'm getting a cold, but I had a feeling of thickness there. I can't help thinking it's linked to my ear problem.

I walked across town to visit Mum and Dad and returned by way of St. John's Church. The Sunday service had finished, but the door was still open so I stepped inside and sat down at the back. I sat there, in private, just for five minutes, then left.

When I got home I flicked on the radio in the kitchen just in time to hear Petula Clark singing *Round Every Corner*. For a brief moment I wondered if you were sending me a signal, but such an outrageous notion soon left me. I have to say though that the words were supremely apt for my current situation.

*****

Sifting through more photographs in the evening reduced me to tears again and I decided to go to bed early.

*****

I had another bad night. I'd woken up just after one and never properly got back to sleep, so I continued to read the little booklet you left for me, *A Catholic Approach To Dying*. That may not sound like an ideal book to read upon waking, but I wanted to cover off everything in it. Besides, what else was I going to do while waiting for the rest of the town to stir? I'd also recently added a library book to my reading list entitled, *You'll Get Over It*, by Virginia Ironside, which I hoped would help me in my grief.

Selfishly, perhaps, I have been hoping that you would come to me. Whether in a dream or that I should see or hear you during all my waking hours, I would not mind. Just to have you back again, if only to glimpse, would be wonderful.

There have been moments just lately when I have thought that you have been trying to get through, but it hasn't happened. Today is our 24th Wedding Anniversary. Might you come to me later tonight?

*****

Darling, if you did pay me a visit, I have to say I didn't see you. After all my unsettled nights I must have slept like a log. Sorry, Doll.

I went to Acorn Ridge. I sat there, in relative peace, noticing only the occasional sound of a vehicle on one of the surrounding roads. Clouds bubbled up in an otherwise clear blue sky, letting the sunlight through to dapple the site. There was very little breeze. It was a day very similar to the one on which we were wed. But as I sat in silence beside you, the unfairness of the situation filled me with deep sadness. I was sad for myself – the survivor – for I knew nothing would ever be the same again. And I was sad for you, my Darling. After you were given the diagnosis last December you fought so hard against the brutal disease. It didn't seem right to think, *'Linda's pain free'* or *'at least she isn't suffering'*. Even knowing that your body absolutely couldn't take any more didn't make it any easier. My hurting, my yearning for you, my pining, crying, physical discomfort, my emptiness, all seemed so intense that I wondered once more if I'd ever recover.

Would I have swapped places with you?

Possibly.

Would I have preferred to have gone with you?

Definitely.

As I sat there, the thought came to me that you would approve of the surroundings. But you're gone. You're not even under this pile of soil (and what a big pile of soil it is, remember, it's the size of a double bed!). That's your body down there, the bit the cancer destroyed, but you're here in my head now and in everyone's head who ever knew you. You're all around. And people will talk about you and keep your memory alive.

I think I am suffering so much right now because I spent all my time with you. I miss you. I always thought that I wouldn't want to go back and sit beside your grave, or any grave, but I was pleased to have come. I was pleased to take away some of the dead and dying flowers and to tidy the mound. I reorganised the remaining floral tributes and placed fresh flowers there with my own message:

'Flowers for my Baby on the day we were wed. I love you, Linda.'

I knew I would come back and I know that I will come back again and again. And yet even as I sat there, the reality was still almost unbelievable.

And unbearable.

*****

I slept until 5.30 a.m. which I thought was good.

I went to the doctor at last. She prescribed some Corsodyl for my throat and asked the practice nurse to syringe my troublesome ear.

I returned to your plot. I know I have called it a 'grave' but, honestly, I'd rather not. 'Grave' has a definite feeling of finality about it. I have no doubt though that one day I will refer to it in such a way. For today at least, 'plot' seems to be a good word to use.

And today I tidied the mound again and planted several packets of bulbs that I'd bought in M&S this morning. I placed the bulbs so as to form a four letter word on the hump, remembering what the rules are about staying within the bounds of the hole. Blimey, how many ways are there to describe your location? When I had finished I sat for a while in the silence. It was certainly a peaceful today, and so warm that it was like a summer's day.

'Make 'em grow, Darling,' I whispered to you. 'Make 'em grow,' I repeated.

They'll spell *LOVE* if they do.

*****

Just as we did when you were very ill, I have Radio Three on in the house these days. I find it comforting most of the time, because it takes my mind back to having you here. But I reach for the 'off' switch when Strauss comes on, or when something else grates on me, such as music that's too lively at six thirty in the morning, or when they play a 'modern' piece that I think is so discordant as to be an affront to listeners. We didn't tolerate that then. I won't put up with it now.

*****

Me, trying to be organised and look efficient: I bought a little Basildon Bond pad, so that I could write thank you notes and so on. In the flyleaf was an offer for 1000 address labels for just £7.99 so I sent off a cheque with my details – just *my* details. These labels, when they come back, will have my name only on them. It was a very strange feeling to know that correspondence for *Mr. and Mrs.* would, ultimately, be no more. And it was another reminder of my present situation.

*****

My sister Jackie, and Colin, Maddie and Billy, were in America at the end of September and we let them know of your passing in a carefully worded text. They also missed your funeral, which was over two weeks ago, so now they were back and the mound was tidier, I organised a graveside service for them and for other family members and friends who hadn't been able to attend. I cleared it with Acorn Ridge, explaining that there would be quite a few people there. My plan was to repeat the church service with the readings and prayers. If I could download good recordings from the internet of the hymns we sang, I would put those on CD and play those too, although I didn't tell Acorn Ridge that.

I read the opening prayer then the first hymn issued from the CD player at a reasonable volume.

John's gospel passage followed. This was John 14:2 and I have heard it at several funerals. I think it was a helpful reading at your service.

The song *I'll Walk Beside You* played through:

I'll walk beside you through the world today
While dreams and songs and flowers bless your way
I'll look into your eyes and hold your hand
I'll walk beside you through the golden land

I'll walk beside you through the world tonight
Beneath the starry skies ablaze with light
And in your heart love's tender words I'll hide
I'll walk beside you through the eventide

I'll walk beside you through the passing years
Through days of cloud and sunshine, joy and tears
And when the great call comes, the sunset gleams
I'll walk beside you to the land of dreams

and then we heard sister Linda's poem:

Through the blackened trees the sun sets its head
down in glory.

With a glow of radiance shining over, offering itself.
For the day had shone with beauty as you slipped peacefully away.

And, as the seasons changed from winter through to autumn,
we watched helplessly as the leaves once again did fall.
Knowing and praying, feeble in our existence.

With the path lit deeply through the trees, a smile succumbed.
For you would not be journeying alone, nor in the dark.
Your pathway unlocked, as you crossed the passages of life.

The beauty of the day shaded with sorrow and mourning.
But the beauty of the day and the sun through the trees, perfect.
Now, beautiful lady, resting and sleeping, you are at peace.

© Linda Seymour

I read Jenni's sonnet aloud:

When she who was the cause of all our sighs,
Withdrew from our world and from our eyes,
Nature itself, was full of sorrow to see,
Men weeping, at the loss of such as she.

But nature may not boast as once it did,
Death by love is conquered: love has laid
This glorious creature with the blessed ones

Thus death, so pitiless, is now deceived
It has no power to harm such perfection
Or dim her triumph, as once it believed.

Love will be shining with her soul's reflection
Since she in death lives abundantly
She would not leave us willingly

Dear to me is sleep, still more
Then do not wake me, keep your voices low

We listened to another hymn, *The King Of Love My Shepherd Is* and said prayers together, reading from the Order Of Service I had printed. After the last hymn, *Guide Me Oh Thou Great Redeemer*, I read a final prayer:

Most merciful God, whose wisdom is beyond
our understanding, surround us with your love,
that we may not be overwhelmed by our loss,
but have confidence in your goodness and
strength to meet the days to come.
We ask this through Christ our Lord.
Amen

And then I pushed 'Play' one last time so that everyone could listen to the Coldplay track.

*****

Acorn Ridge contacted me last week to let me know that your stone was ready and to ask if I would like to be there when it went down. I thought it was an invitation I shouldn't decline and so I arranged to meet Cheryl, from Acorn Ridge, at the burial site at 10.00 a.m. today. She was already there and had cut a turf, about 300mm square, from the ground at the head of your plot. She asked me if I would prefer to be left alone and lay the stone myself, so that's what I did.

The stone looked good and the words that were cut into it said everything. You'll always be 'Wagamama'; you'll always be loved; and you won't grow old as those who are left will.

The weather was fantastic, with blue sky, sunshine and a very light breeze. You would have called it the *'breeze in the trees'* just as in one of your poems. The trees themselves showed off beautiful autumn colour, with red, gold and yellow. It was a perfect day for setting your stone in the ground; to put your name next to an otherwise anonymous pile of earth there at Acorn Ridge.

My first attempt failed when I realised the stone was rocking on the bed of sand I had laid.

'For goodness sake,' I muttered, 'you've laid a patio but you can't lay this stone? Come on.'

I scolded myself for my poor first attempt.

When I did finish I was initially pleased with it, then wondered if I'd left the stone a bit high. I wanted to check with Cheryl, but when I looked up I found myself alone at the site. I hadn't even seen her leave.

'Oh, well,' I mumbled, 'either the mower will clip it or they'll re-bed it to their standards.'

I sat on the nearest bench, looked around, considered my surroundings and why I was there then reminded myself of the words on the stone:

LINDA PAGE
'WAGAMAMA'
Forever loved,
forever young

Loneliness once more overwhelmed me and I began to cry.

On my way home, I passed two riders on horseback and suddenly recalled part of a song I'd once tried to write – first when Grandad died and then again when Karl died. It went something like:

You saddled up your chestnut mare
And smiled a goodbye smile
And we could only watch
As you turned and rode away

I haven't ever finished it, but then I started thinking about another song: Jimmy MacCarthy's *Ride On*. As the words came to me, I realised I was making sense of a song that I have been singing for years.

*****

It's now exactly one month since you died. My grief is raw and unrelenting.

Back at home I checked my emails. Alec had sent an email to the members of the band, to remind us of the booking at the local pub in a week or so. He wondered if I felt up to joining in, but was also understanding of my situation.

I'm not sure about singing and playing, but I will at least help Alec with setting up.

*****

I had a follow up appointment at the surgery with my GP this morning. My ear, although it has been syringed, continues to give me discomfort and my tongue is still black. The Corsodyl hasn't worked, but I am still trying the pineapple cure, which I described to the doctor. She had not heard or read of it, but I assured her that I would persevere.

Later the same day I had an eye test at one of the opticians in town. The 'pressures' in my eyes were measured using a puff of air that made me jump each time. I was told the pressures were high and I would now have to be referred to my GP. And my prescription is different, too. Blimey, Doll, I seem to be falling apart – quite literally!

*****

I received a letter today from one of the key people involved with us this past year. When you were ill, they called both of us by our first names and they were always professional, polite and friendly. Their personal approach, in addition to the treatment and care we had, did much to ease our ongoing and deteriorating situation. Of course, they were there for you, but I also took some comfort from their attitude to us as a couple dealing with cancer. I liked the person.

But this letter annoyed me – I mean, *really* annoyed me. I was immediately irritated to see, at the top, that they had started it *Dear Mr. Page*. My displeasure didn't end there. They had written:

> *It is now some weeks since your bereavement and we are thinking of you.*
> *We enclose a leaflet about bereavement which we hope you will find helpful at this difficult time.*

*Please feel free to contact us again if you need
further information or advice.
With best wishes...*

In disbelief, I considered the style and content of the letter. What had happened to that personal approach? In what way did they think that this letter would be helpful to me? I felt jilted. The letter made me think that because you had died, I was now merely a loose end that had to be tied up. I know they were there primarily for you, I know that, but I also thought they were there for me, so the formality of the correspondence rankled me.

They had included leaflets with the letter, with information on bereavement counselling. At the time, I didn't want them and I was annoyed that they had been sent to me because I think seeing them made me feel I wasn't coping. Maybe I wasn't. Perhaps some tittle-tattle had got round to them that Chris Page is struggling and could do with a lift. Regardless of how I was coping, the letter and enclosures only angered me and lowered my self-esteem. The contents of their envelope were the antithesis of what I needed right then.

After I'd calmed down, I thought about the position they were in and I forgave them their thoughtlessness. It was always going to be difficult for them to strike a balance. I mean, they couldn't carry on being chummy with me indefinitely. At some point they would have to let me go and leave me to face up to my future. The person wasn't my pen pal and it was inevitable that my relationship with them would cease.

*****

I have continued with my picture project and started to make a montage – at least, I think that's what it's called. I must have heard the expression before and it definitely sounds like what I'm doing. The photographs I am gathering are going to go in clip frames. The frames are large, A2 size, and the photos I have been printing are the size of tea cards (if we could still get tea cards) or like those bubble gum cards that I remember collecting as a boy. Most of the photos are those taken on our little pocket Nikon, but some are from Wayne and Sara's camera. Others have been clipped from the internet or else scanned in to our computer so that I can print them off. What have I clipped from the internet? I have a picture of The George at Vernham Dean and one of the Ivy in West Street. The scans are of the business card from The Mayfly at Chilbolton and of a flyer that came with some cake that Sara bought you. It reads, 'Too much is never enough'. When it comes to cake or chocolate, I probably agree. No, I *do* agree.

Most of the photographs are ours though, those taken after your diagnosis and which record both highs and lows. There are pictures of parties, family and friends and of new additions to family or friends. There are magical moments shared between the two of us, such as The New Forest and the Enchanted Manor, our private time in the Crow's Nest or just resting downstairs. The lows, even as I study the photographs, are low points for me, not you. You had the remarkable ability to smile through the most appalling pain, immobility and setback, your glass always half-full, mine almost empty at times. My lows, and I worry that I will forget – I don't ever want to forget – are centred on the unfairness of it all. I can see pictures of you with your wonderful smile, but I can also see the cancer, the treatment and, I have to say, the 'journey' we all made and the destination. My low now is being here without you. I wonder if I will ever learn to cope without you.

And so these photographs, each just 8cm x 6cm and printed in colour, are currently in a loose pile. These images must be sorted, graded. Before I forget. In case I forget. Never mind that photo paper and ink cartridges are so expensive, I am driven, desperate to create this montage, desperate to hold on to you. I have three borderless clip frames. I'm sure that is enough, and I have worked out that I should get 42 pictures, *tea cards*, in each one.

*****

Linda, I am very happy to tell you that the pineapple cure seems to have worked! I stuck with it and my tongue is looking much better now. It's good to knock something off the 'worry list' at last.

*****

I wrote to our friends in Australia:

This is just a short letter to accompany the contents of the envelope.

I hope you're all well. We're kind of okay, inasmuch as we don't have any colds or flu but we're grieving for Linda. It's still only been a few weeks since she died and some days I think I expect too much of myself. Most days I think I will never recover, but I know 'these things happen' all the time and that people do learn to live with their grief. I find that talking about what's happened (and writing, too) helps a lot.

One of my sisters was abroad with her family and we broke the news to them in a text. When she returned she asked if we could run through the funeral service at the graveside, so we did. I've enclosed the Order of Service from the funeral, but also put in the little service that I 'ministered' up on the hill. Altogether that day there were ~~seventeen~~ (eighteen – forgot to include myself) around the grave. My Mum said it helped her and a peace descended upon her which continues to give her strength.

I've also put in some photographs – some old, some new. The flowers you sent were stunning and I was reduced to tears when I took delivery and read your beautiful words. Thank you all very much. Beside the flowers [in the photo] is a mock up of a magazine cover that Wayne and Sara did for my birthday last year using a favourite photo of Linda. When they gave it to me I burst out crying! I'm an accomplished bawler these days and never know when the tears will come. They just do.

I know Mum has already sent you some pictures of our 'Wedding Vows' day back in June, but I've put some in anyway. In particular I wanted to show you the heart shape that the balloons formed as we let them go that evening. Apart from two stragglers, it was uncanny – magical even – that this happened. It was indeed a special day.

During the month that followed our service, Linda's health deteriorated. She fought to the very end and even writing this down now I can feel tears of sadness stinging my eyes.

As I said in my last letter, I have been writing a great deal this year. I hope to be able to transcribe my jottings into something resembling a book, although I've no idea if that will take months or years.
Anyway, I'm going to close now. And I know Christmas is going to be difficult. It always brings a bit of 'Bah, humbug' out in me anyway, but I'm going to have to be strong. With the love and support of family and friends we will all move on.

Love to you all.
You're all very special to me.
Chris
xx

*****

When I told you I wanted a belly bar, to go with my other piercings, you thought I was crazy. You couldn't understand why anyone would want one, much less a bloke. Well, today I went and got my navel pierced. It wasn't as painful as I thought it might be and was all done in minutes. But I have to take care of it now while it heals, which could take several weeks.

And I'll bet you still think I'm crazy!

*****

Today I received my official invitation to Emma and Mikee's wedding next April. I know Emma had brought forward her hen party so that you could join her, and I remember how determined you were to make it. That was just six months ago.

The R.S.V.P. was something of a questionnaire. It was an uncomfortable feeling, completing it in the singular. I am desolate without you and even replying has been a test of strength. I know I must go on without you. I will attend the wedding.

Guests have been invited to choose a song, to be played during the day, and I have chosen *'So Do I'*, sung by Christy Moore. I don't expect the D.J. to have this, so I have sent back my reply and enclosed a copy of the track on a CD. The song was one you loved to hear me sing, and we both liked the words and the tune. I checked it after I had put it on to the disc and I was moved to tears because of everything the song meant to us. Listening to it also brought you close to me again but, as always at such times, left you just out of my reach. So that I could make contact I closed my eyes and imagined you next to me, touching me, your breath on my cheek and the scent of you all around. I love you and miss you, my Darling.

*****

Oh, what a mess the funeral directors have created. I contacted them today to ask if I could come in to pick up the donations because I want to pass them on to The Berkshire Cancer Centre before Christmas.

'You collected them on Monday.' The person on the other end of the phone was polite and assured. It was a very matter-of-fact response.

Now, I know it's only been a couple of months since you went away and my head is far from okay, but I would remember picking up something so important. I was immediately concerned that the charitable donations had been stolen. How could this happen? To who were they released?

'No, I haven't been in,' I said.

'Well someone's collected the envelope, because it was here and now it's not.'

'Did you get a signature?'

'Oh, we don't get people to sign.'

The phone became muffled as the person taking my call passed on my comments to someone else there. I couldn't properly make out the responses but the consensus in the office was that Mr. Page had collected the envelope.

I told them again that I hadn't been in and expressed my dismay that the donations hadn't been signed for.

'Perhaps your friend picked up the envelope?' They referred to our friend, who works for the funeral director.

'No. He would have told me.'

Under normal circumstances, the funeral director would send donations to the nominated charity. I've been the fly in the ointment here, because I wanted to take them personally. I wasn't being awkward, Dolly. It was just that I wanted to top up the funds. Although they already amounted to a considerable sum of money, I wanted to boost the donations to a specific figure that I had in my mind.

When we put the notice of your funeral in the paper, we had asked *'No flowers please. Donations to The Berkshire Cancer Centre.'*

Cheques and cash came in with sympathy cards. At the church, because I had already paid for the service, all of the retiring collection was for the Centre. The donations were counted and passed to the funeral directors. I gave all the cheques and other cash I had to them. Any further donations went straight to the funeral directors. It was something else I didn't have to worry about.

I was worried now, though. Assurances that everything would be fine did not, in the circumstances, settle my mind. I asked the contact at the funeral directors for figures and how they were going to resolve the matter. The cash, they said, was easy, as they had converted it all into a single cheque. They would cancel that and write another one. All of the other cheques – and there were a lot of them – were a different matter. They would send a letter to everyone who had made out a cheque, asking them to cancel it and do another one. They made it sound simple and perhaps they thought it was. Then *I* thought that perhaps this has happened to them before. The reality turned out to be a nightmare, for me and for some of your family and friends.

The funeral directors had a record of all the cheques they had received and gave me a list of names. I was asked to provide contact details for the people on the list and I managed to do so with only a few exceptions.

The letters went out.

Many people, when they received their letter, got in touch with me instead of the funeral directors, concerned that they were being scammed or defrauded. It was then for me to explain what had happened, try to reassure them and at the same time suppress my embarrassment. I couldn't believe what had happened and, even though it wasn't my fault, I felt awkward. I imagined some of the donors wondering what kind of service the professionals were providing.

During this fiasco, I had to say something to the funeral directors so that it wouldn't happen to anyone else.

'You need to look at your process controls. You can't just let someone walk off with a bag full of money without getting a signature or a receipt.'

Obvious really!

*****

The process of sending out letters and getting replacement cheques from our kind donors was slow and I was sure now that I wouldn't be able to take the final amount to the Berkshire Cancer Centre this side of Christmas. Have a look here at what the funeral directors put in their letter:

> *Dear...*
> *You recently were kind enough to send a cheque as a donation to The Berkshire Cancer Centre, in memory of Mrs Page.*
> *Unfortunately, the envelope containing the donations has not been delivered to Mr Page, so we are in the process of contacting everyone to ask if it would be possible for them to replace their cheques.*
> *We are very sorry for any inconvenience and distress caused by this. Please would you be kind enough to send us a replacement cheque, in the envelope provided?*

Please do not hesitate to contact us if you have any questions.
Assuring you of our best attentions at all times.
Yours
(Funeral Directors)

Well, I wonder what you'd have to say about it, Darling. Me? I'm disappointed beyond measure.

For one thing, they didn't give anyone, least of all me, their *best attentions* when it came to the donations, but they also worded the letter in such a way that they took absolutely no responsibility for losing the money. I know, I'm ranting again. But I hope you can understand my frustration.

Anyway, there's nothing else I can do to speed things up. I'm just going to have to wait a bit longer.

*****

I went to the bank today, Doll. The mortgage centre had sent me a Redemption Statement a few days ago and whilst part of the money owing on our house was paid by the insurance we had in place, there was still a substantial amount outstanding.

I didn't get past the reception desk, from where a young woman – a school leaver perhaps, certainly only in her teens – asked if she could help. I explained my purpose and she said it was something she could do there. I saw that Aldo was standing behind her. Remember I told you about him a few weeks ago? He had made the account changes for me. I greeted him in recognition, wondered fleetingly if he was training her, but allowed the young woman to process my requirements. She called up my accounts on her computer screen and moved our money around.

'It must be a lovely feeling to be paying off your mortgage,' she said, looking up at me.

One corner of my mouth twitched, but I couldn't quite manage a smile. Aldo took a short step forward, leaned down and whispered something in her ear.

'Oh, I'm sorry,' she said to me.

And then I felt a little bit sorry for her and gave forgiveness by telling her it was okay.

I hope it was a lesson well learned and I was grateful for Aldo's presence at this sad but terribly important moment in the aftermath of your passing.

*****

It's the start of the weekend, but I had another eye test this morning with a different high street optician.

I've been back to the other opticians several times since my eye test three weeks ago and I'm not happy with them. As well as recording raised pressure in my eyes, when my new prescription glasses arrived I couldn't see properly out of them. I was told that my eyes would adjust to the new lenses. With doubt in my mind I duly took them home and tried them for a few days. They were useless. I took them back and again explained that I couldn't see with the new glasses. The assistant put the new glasses into a focimeter and assured me the lenses were the right prescription and – which seemed very important for him to stress to me – they were *Zeiss lenses*. He would send them back to the lab to be checked. When I returned, nothing had changed.

'You might as well keep them,' I said, 'because as far as I'm concerned they're just an ornament. I can't wear them.'

At this morning's eye test, I was hoping that I would end up with a functioning prescription. But I'd also gone because I thought if the other optician could mess up my glasses, perhaps they had also messed up the measurement of the pressures within my eyes.

The puff of air made me jump, as always.

The pressures were not within normal range and a letter would have to be sent to my GP. Blast it! Now the doctor's going to get two letters saying the same thing. And now I can't help but wonder if I will end up with glaucoma, like Pa.

*****

I walked up to Acorn Ridge. It took me exactly one hour and ten minutes. I hadn't been for two weeks. When I got to you I found that 'the hump' had started to collapse and I guessed the wicker coffin had finally given way under the weight of the earth above it and, probably, a natural process was well under way.

I'll be back soon, with some soil and some tools, to try to even out some of the sinking. I hope I don't disturb the daffodil bulbs then.

*****

I sat on the sofa. I was sad and I was feeling sorry for myself. Loneliness washed over me, just as it has so many times before. I looked around at the photographs, the room, the drapery, at our house. As my gaze and my mind broadened their viewpoint, I got mad again. Tears welled up in my puffy eyes and I let out a plea.

'Oh, Darling, Darling, what am I going to do?' I asked out loud, looking across at your photograph on the mantel shelf.

Then a teardrop fell onto my shirt and I sat there wondering selfishly what was to become of me, the person left behind. Self-pity soon turned to anger and in rage I thumped the sofa hard with both fists.

'I don't want you to be dead,' I shouted out, through gritted teeth.

But it counted for nothing because I can't change what has happened. You are gone from me and I am going to have to find a way of coping without you. Somehow, too, I am going to have to cope with the range of emotions I find myself facing every day.

Physically, of course, I can do a lot of the stuff we did as a team: I cook, wash, keep house, and change the bedclothes. And, although I'm not as good at it as you and I don't have much interest in it right now, I can even work in the garden if I have to. What I struggle with, certainly at the moment anyway, is my very existence, when all I really want is to be with you.

*****

My referral to the ophthalmologist clinic at the local hospital was turned round promptly and I was thoroughly checked out today. Just as we both did when you were ill, I wanted to know what was going on and I asked questions. I passed the visual fields test. This was good news at last. It's one of the tests that can detect the early signs of glaucoma. And my pressures were checked this time with a contact tonometer. Instead of the frightening readings in the 20s that the puff test had found, the pressures were recorded at 16 and 17.

A reading of 15 is regarded as normal; anything above 21 or 22 is cause for concern.

The clinic will see me in one year for a further review.

*****

Our Internet Service Provider sent out a blanket e-mail tonight, trying to encourage their customers to take up broadband, phone line and calls in one easy package. If I signed up to an eighteen-month contract I could make the most of a great deal.

I replied to them:

> *Dear Internet Service Provider,*
> *I just did all this.*
> *My new contract started yesterday. Why have you sent me the information? Do your records show something different?*

Within ten minutes they came back to me:

> *Dear customer,*
> *Sorry, but unfortunately we won't be able to reply to your e-mail.*
> *To contact us please* [go to our website].
> *Kind regards,*
> *Customer Services*

Customer Services?! How can they send out an invitation like that? It's like *Knock Down Ginger* by email.

It was, of course, an unmonitored mailbox. I knew that, but it didn't stop me ticking about it.

*****

I feel that I am right back to dreading the night time again. I know that if I go to bed too early I won't sleep, but all this going to bed late is catching up with me. I am exhausted. Anyway, tonight, after a cup of tea and a read, hopefully I'll get a good night's rest.

I went to bed at 11.15 p.m. and woke at 6.15 a.m. I reckoned that was pretty good.

*****

The run up to Christmas was predictably difficult. I was never really much of a Christmas person at the best of times. You and Wayne were always much better at it. I was always glad to see the back of it although, in my defence, I think that's because the event rarely met my expectations. For me, it's an annual six-month trial. My misery starts in September, when the supermarkets begin to stock family tins of *Quality Street* and giant *Toblerone*. They put their puddings and pies out, their mincemeat and ready-to-roll pastry. Those irritating and cheesy Christmas songs start to play over the sound system. The same songs, year after year, seep into one's subconscious and torture my brain. Cards then swell the aisles, shelf after shelf of charity cards, cheap cards and luxury cards. Tinsel and glitter sparkle beneath huge banners that read 'Seasonal Goods'. When Christmas is still three months away – one quarter of a year away – we are drawn into thinking about it and start spending money that some of us can ill afford. Before long, every shop in town follows suit. On a full shopping day, I have heard the entire top twenty cheesy Christmas songs as I have gone from one retailer to another.

Then there are the decorations. The tree: do we get a real one, or get that ten-year-old artificial tree out of the attic again? Oh, the attic. What a deep joy it is, to go crawling on my hands and knees into that dark and dusty place, pulling a whole load of stuff out just so that I can get to the Christmas boxes that have been put to the back. These are the boxes that contain a lifetime's collection of Christmas decorations: glass baubles wrapped in toilet tissue, some so fragile they may not survive the festive season, clip-on birds and berries, strings of pearls, angel hair and, of course, tinsel in great quantity. More than anyone else, you know that decorating the tree has always been one of my least favourite Christmas activities, probably because I dread taking it all down afterwards. And then I have to put it back in the attic for the next 350 days.

Another thing that annoys me is that we put ourselves through this twelve-week ordeal for the sake of an hour or so of opening presents on Christmas morning. After that, it's all over. Boxing Day is the official 'get over it' day, then it's business as usual and for the next twelve weeks we try to claw our finances back to where they were before.

That's the commercial side of Christmas. That's the bit I don't really like these days. In the past, I tolerated it and I have wondered, year after year, why it annoys me more as I get older.

For all my moaning, I do try, if only a little, to muster some festive spirit. You and I would spend hours, night after night, writing cards to friends and family. Many of our cards would include notes about what we had been doing. We would sometimes put in a long letter if we had a lot to say or hadn't seen the recipient for a long time. Remember last year? We didn't send many cards out because you were so ill. You weren't expected to see Christmas, things were that bad. I got up in the attic then, without complaining. I even assembled the trusty old tree in the lounge and brought down all the decorations so that you, Wayne and Sara could decorate it. You all did a great job. I cried.

I cried again this year, too. Something as simple as wrapping presents made me sad. We had a system. One or the other would hold down the paper as the other applied sticky tape. Buying and wrapping was a joint venture. We did everything together. Now it's just me and I'd rather not be doing any of it.

I will push on though, Darling, and get on with life as best I can. But don't think I'm going all out with the decorations again.

*****

The day before Christmas Eve this year I ran away to the Gower peninsula to spend Christmas on my own. It's the first Christmas since your passing. I could not bear to have to pretend that everything was fine. To have to smile and laugh my way through a Christmas Day in anyone's company was not what I wanted. As hard as it was, I had decided to go it alone. You, Wayne and I had holidayed in Gower and we loved it, but I knew no one there.

After driving more than a hundred and fifty miles, I reached the sea at Port Eynon just as the light faded. My hotel was just behind the dunes. I was its only guest over Christmas and I was a stranger in town.

At eight o'clock on Christmas Eve I returned to my hotel room after Christmas Holy Communion at

St. Cattwg's, in the village. You and I often went to midnight mass. I still felt an urge to go.

The service was well attended. The church was warm and cosy and the people welcoming of all. For these reasons, and one more, it was an experience I shall not forget, for the Reverend Canon Joe Griffin was totally blind. I only realised this when, at the beginning of the service, he asked the Churchwarden to light the fifth Advent candle and tell him when he had done so.

At the altar rail he depended upon the congregation to reach out for the bread instead of him passing it to them. Navigating his way along the row of people waiting for bread and wine, he eventually came to me.

'Non-communicant, Father', I respectfully explained when I realised he was waiting for my outstretched hand.

'What is your name?' he asked.

'Chris', I replied.

'Chris', he said, 'may the Lord Jesus bless you and keep you. Amen.'

At the end of the whole evening he made his way to the door as we all sang the last carol and there he waited to shake the hand of everyone who had attended the service. It was a small, 12th Century church, but the congregation filled it, so leaving the building took a while.

When I reached him I took his hand and gave it a gentle squeeze, wishing him a happy and peaceful Christmas. He must have remembered my voice from the Eucharist.

'Where are you from', he asked.

'Newbury.'

'I've a friend who once worked in Newbury. George Bennett. He moved to Newton. Did you know him?'

I could hardly believe what I'd heard and he could probably sense the shock in my reply.

'Father George married me', I said, proudly. 'Gosh, what a small world.'

'Yes, indeed', he agreed. 'He's now Canon of Brecon Cathedral. I'll tell him when I see him that I met someone who knows him. What's your name?'

'Chris', I replied, stupidly, because I knew he already knew that.

'I'm sure he's come across a few Chris's.'

'Sorry', I said, 'Chris Page'. I was holding up the queue, but I left the church feeling extremely lifted. It was definitely an enchanted moment and I got that feeling again that there was magic about.

I passed my account to Wayne and Sara by way of email later the same evening.

*****

They replied early on Christmas morning.

Friday, 0800hrs
From: Wayne
Subject: Truly amazing!

We're all loving this.

It sounds like you're getting everything you were looking for out of your little adventure, and more. I checked my little weather service out and it tells me that you should have a fair old bit of sunshine today (rain the rest of the week, mind!). Mama's definitely with you.

*And she's already made her presence known
here too:
Sara and Katie were putting out the place mats
for breakfast and, from who knows where, a little
white feather landed between mine and Sara's
mats. I think there'll be seven of us
sitting down for breakkie this morning!*

*Enjoy your day - please don't feel that you have
to go out of your way to find a call box - your
time and solitude there is precious.*

*Well, Happy Christmas, Popsie. Everyone here
sends their fondest love. I'm so very proud of
you for the way you've come through the year,
and the love and support you've given me too.*

*I love you very much.
Speak soon,
Wayne xxx*

I got to Oxwich Bay at 10.20 a.m. on Christmas Day
by way of a ruined castle and a nature reserve and met a
man at the bay car park who was walking his dog. He
was the first person I'd seen on my walk that morning.

'Can I get to the sea this way?' I asked him.

'Yes. It's straight through there,' he said, almost in
disbelief that he should be talking to someone on the
peninsular who didn't know that. 'You can't miss it,' he
went on. 'It's bluer than the sky today.' His local accent
seemed to emphasise everything he said.

I concurred with him that the weather was fantastic
before parting company and making my way to the bay.

Moments later I was sitting on the beach eating a mince pie, drinking Highland Spring water and soaking up warm sunshine under a clear, blue sky. Just as the man in the car park had told me, the sea was bluer than the sky. In a slow and gentle rhythm, it flopped lazily onto the shore and as I cast my gaze from one side of the bay to the other, the whole scene was stunning. It was a very strange feeling to be sitting in the sun on a UK beach on Christmas Day. Then I reminded myself of what I'd said long before I'd got away, which was that this Christmas was always going to be memorable or, rather, to use your word, *'memoriable'*. I can't remember when you first coined that phrase, but I like to use it from time to time because it is yours. It is you and it brings you back to me, if only for a moment.

When I got back to the hotel, I calculated that I'd walked just seven miles, but the going had been extremely difficult, with lots of claggy mud and very steep climbs and descents. It had been worth the effort.

*****

It's very rare that you come to me in a dream, but last night you did. It all seems weird this Boxing Day morning anyway, and I can't make sense of it:

> *I think I had a job, which may have been with my previous employer, but which may not. I think you had a job, which may have been on the District, but which may not. We had the white Vauxhall Carlton estate (we sold that at least five years ago) and you called me on the mobile to arrange to meet. Something had held me up and you called again to ask where I was and how*

long I'd be. I assured you I was on the way and I recall making my way over some wooden formwork that had been put in place during the construction of some kind of building. You know I don't do heights, but I had no issues with crawling over this high level structure and didn't care what the workmen thought of my intrusion. My bigger problem was that I simply could not remember where I had parked the car. I'm fairly sure you knew where the car was and that you were waiting there for me, but I couldn't get to you because I didn't know where to go.

Ultimately, the distress I was suffering as a result of knowing that you were close, that I would soon see you, but couldn't locate you, woke me up.

Then I wondered if I could remember where I'd parked the Ford Focus. Oh, yes, right outside the hotel.

It may have been a dream, but it may not.

*****

After a bad night, the combined result of stormy weather blowing hard at the window, rain lashing down on the roof (I was in one of the roof bedrooms) and my dream of you, I eventually got up at a ridiculous hour and made a cup of tea. I had shaved, showered and was all done and dressed by 6.45 a.m.

I began to tidy things up, wanting to leave the place as I'd found it. I wiped all the surfaces, made sure the bed was as crease-free as possible then made sure I cleaned the shower tray and wash basin. I washed up crockery and cutlery as I went along, swept the all-wood floors to clear the mud and sand I'd walked in on my boots. After suggesting, three days ago, that I would leave at around eleven, I was now thinking of getting away early. Perhaps even before nine.

The sink blockage that I'd caused last night by trying to wash rice away was thankfully clear. I had rodded out the waste pipe using the aerial from my portable radio. I managed to break the aerial entirely, but at least I didn't have to call the man. In addition to all the work I was doing this morning, last night I'd also emptied the trap beneath the sink at least four times, having first removed the under-sink cupboard contents, and then completely wiping the inside of the cupboard before putting everything back tidily.

The waste bin contained some of last night's rice, a little leftover curry, the broken radio aerial and a couple of empty beer cans. I couldn't let the man see that, so I even emptied the contents of my pedal bin into the big bin downstairs.

I felt like a perpetrator trying to wipe evidence from the scene of a crime.

But I had managed to get through Christmas.

Having made such an early start, my drive east was clear and I was back at home before lunch.

*****

As I left our local, the old year disappeared.

I announced the new one to two young men who were sprawled out on the pub's bench seats outside. I could hardly believe what I was saying. The old year had to have been the worst one of my life, and it had to have been for you, too, Darling.

I miss you so much.

I looked up at a full moon, which was high and bright in the clear night sky.

Fireworks were going off all across town, although I could only hear them. I didn't see any.

'So, here we are, then,' I mumbled. 'The new year's come.'

I hadn't swapped 'Happy New Year' with anyone except the two lads outside the pub. As soon as I got home, I unlocked the back doors and went out into the garden. I sat on the bench by the shed and marvelled at just what an amazing moon it was and at how the entire garden was aglow under its light.

Then I went to bed.

Two

When I eventually went downstairs, the New Year was already seven and a half hours old.

I found my mobile phone with its cover off and the battery on the bathroom floor. I also saw half a cup of tea on the side and blood on the bathroom door. Chunks of skin were missing from the knuckles on my right hand and I tried to piece together in my mind what had happened. I knew I'd had a few drinks the night before. I was feeling the effects now.

I remembered being angry when I got home last night because I'm here and you're there, and I don't like it. I don't want you to be dead. It isn't fair. Then I remembered that I'd vented my frustration by launching a frenzied attack on a few inanimate objects. Needless to say, it didn't help and I had come off worse.

'Happy New Year', I thought.

I was still so loaded with alcohol that morning that I cycled to Acorn Ridge. I certainly couldn't drive. It was a crisp but clear morning, a beautiful day in fact on which to start the New Year. The cycling was strenuous for me and I got off and pushed a couple of times because I couldn't do it.

Two cyclists called out to me as I was coasting past Hamstead Park.

'Ice!' they yelled. 'Right across the road! Take care!'

I owe them a debt of gratitude. The driver of the abandoned car in the ditch had not had such a warning. An ambulance passed me, silently, carefully, but on blue lights, and it pulled up at the pub just ahead. The thought occurred to me that the car driver had been taken from the scene of his accident to the nearest occupied building.

*****

Remember my long wheelbase Land Rover, Darling? 'Martha' was a 1970 Station Wagon. I hadn't had it long when I met you. We went on our first date with Martha. I lavished care and attention on her and the vehicle was my pride and joy. It was only after I had bought mine that I began to notice all the other Land Rovers on the roads, even though they had always been there.

It wasn't until I was widowed that I saw other widowed men and women around me. Just as one Land Rover was different to the next, so the circumstances and emotions of these widows and widowers differed among them. However, like Land Rovers, they all had a badge that identified them.

Now, I have the badge too.

*****

What were we thinking, Doll, when we did what we did, went where we went, saw what we saw? Why did we go back to the Isle of Wight? Why Blenheim, Spinnaker Tower, the London Eye? Why were these places – and more – on the 'wish list'? For us they weren't, any of them, particularly spectacular, although they were all enjoyable, so what was the attraction? Perhaps they were already on our wish list of places to go and things to do and, in the course of a normal lifetime, we might have got around to some of them.

When we only had months in which to enjoy any of them together, we had to cram them in while you were well enough. Unfortunately, that wasn't always the case. You were often so unwell at times that you could barely walk, were constantly tired and full of fluid. But you pushed on. You would not be denied experiences.

I will never know what memories you took with you, but I hope they are happy memories of the places you visited and the people you met.

*****

I'm going to add to our 'list', Darling. Don't get upset, but I'm making plans to go to America. I'm going to see Deirdre and Leroy, Carl and Fran and Roger and Hermione. That's a lot to cram in because although they're all in the top right of the country, they're in different states. I think I can do it, so now I need to sort out some dates that work for everyone. I'm going to be busy.

My passport runs out in a couple of months.

I applied for a new one today.

*****

I've been looking around the house and garden and I can see all the jobs that I never quite finished; jobs that I should close off. For example, the three four-panel doors downstairs are still just bare wood and they have to be primed, rubbed down, undercoated and top-coated. I don't know what colour they ought to be, but I think it'll be something off-white rather than brilliant white. I know I should replace the carpet threshold strip at the top of the stairs. The one that's there is screwed down through the carpet, but the screws always,

always, jabbed at our feet if we didn't pay the utmost attention. I've been meaning to change it for one that's screwed down underneath the carpet, so there is a smooth bar across the threshold. Then there are the holes above the new curtains at the patio doors. I did fill them, honestly I did. Now I need to sand and paint over the area, but to do that I will have to take down the pelmet and curtains. It's all too complicated. You would never let me sand the wall with the curtains in place – and quite right, too. I know I could do it with your help, but not alone, not now anyway. And the apple tree needs pruning before the end of February. And I still need to install the garden trellis and the rose arch we always said we'd have half way down, just the other side of the apple tree. I've also wanted to install two, six-foot fence panels next to the pergola and plant some bigger stuff there. And what about the patio containers? The list feels endless and onerous.

I know I ought to try to do something, but the truth is I can't get motivated to do anything. Any get up and go I had has evaporated, now that you're not here.

The house was ours and, as such, it was our project, not mine. I can't help feeling that I have lost the incentive to carry on with it. What will I do? Do I stay put and finish the jobs? Do I finish the jobs and move, or not bother with anything and move anyway? I don't know what to do, but I know I have no interest right now. On that basis, perhaps it's as well to do nothing.

*****

I wrote this for '*Bright Lights and Fairy Dust*' because, as you know, I wasn't always the man that people thought I was.

'He wasn't much of a communicator, leaving that to Linda; he rarely checked the calendar for birthdays or appointments; was often as stubborn as a mule – a trait that seemed inherent in the males in his family – and he was always the pessimist. He would only do what he wanted to and didn't like being backed into a corner and, when Chris thought he was simply being serious, Linda thought him grumpy. He rarely enthused about Christmas and Linda would get quite irritated when he didn't get excited at opening presents. He hated the tumble drier (with a passion) and if he got too close would often switch it off to ease the pain on his ears, much to her disgust. The two of them were, very often, as different as chalk and cheese, and yet they totally adored one another. Chris always liked the fact that Linda was strong-willed and assertive and he loved her sense of fun and humour, but when she was on his case he sometimes wondered what it was that she liked about him.

The reality was that she liked his sense of humour too, and they were definitely matched in that regard. And she was always so proud of his achievements: his art, his writing, his music, his woodwork. She was especially proud of him for turning her ideas for the house into reality. Linda had the vision, Chris would sketch her thoughts onto paper and, if she liked what she saw, she would give the go ahead.'

In the end I decided not to put this in but, had I done so, the heading was going to be 'Bastard Man', your name for me when I was being awkward, ridiculous or just plain moody.

*****

This evening we received an e-mail from our ISP or, rather, you did, because it was addressed *'Dear Mrs Page'*.

It was headed up, *Mrs Page, reward yourself with unlimited money off your* [phone] *bill.*

They felt you deserved to be rewarded for the money you spend, so they wanted you to apply for a credit card online. This was despite the fact that I had been in touch with them a month earlier to explain what had happened to you last year. The offer was great: every time you used the credit card they would wipe a bit off the phone bill. And there was no limit! Can you believe that? All you had to do, in order to enjoy the fantastic savings, was apply online. You could do it right then; it would only take you a few minutes and they would get straight back to you with a decision.

I was extremely irritated, not least because this wasn't the first communication that had come from them even after I'd told them the situation. I steamed about it over the weekend then chose to reply by e-mail, even though it was likely to be another unmonitored mailbox. I increased the font size a bit – but not too much – and wrote six words in reply: *Mrs. Page died four months ago.*

'Take that and choke on it,' I muttered as I pressed *Send*.

It was a bit of a bombshell, to be honest, to be made aware that four months have passed since you died.

*****

Today I went to the Berkshire Cancer Centre with the donations that the funeral directors have gathered. I wanted to come before Christmas but, as I told you earlier, Darling, they made a mess of the donations. I also confused them because I wanted to bring the money personally. The normal procedure is for the funeral directors to send the donations; cut everyone else out. But we never did normal, did we?

So, I have the total from everyone who donated in your memory but – and this is important to me – I have added to it to get to the figure I am bringing in today. My brother, when I told him in the week how much we had managed to raise for the Berkshire Cancer Centre, laughed out loud and asked who it was had put in the odd 9p. When I told him it was me and I explained the significance among the numbers, he understood.

I presented £2,709.09.

The date of your passing.

*****

There have already been a few 'firsts': our Wedding Anniversary; Christmas; my Birthday; New Year. Now I was approaching the first Valentine's and I thought back to our last, when we stayed at the Elmers Court Hotel. That was only a couple of months after the dreadful diagnosis and by then you had already taken a dose of radiotherapy for brain metastases.

I treasure all of the cards and notes that you have ever given me, but your last Valentine's card is particularly special:

> *My Darling CP,*
> *I have loved every moment of my life with you.*

I thank you for all your deepest love and
support.
One day, we'll be together forever.
I love you sooo......very much
it hurts me deep inside,
but that is true love.
xxxxxxxxxxxxx

Whenever I'm in the supermarket (*our* supermarket) and I am in the greetings cards aisle, my eyes are drawn to the cards for couples. Those that read 'To my Wife', 'For my Wonderful Wife', 'For my Husband', are so often such beautiful cards that I don't even have to read them for the memory of all those that you and I shared in our time together to come flooding back. I cry too much in the greetings cards aisle. Even selecting a birthday card for a friend or family member will set me off these days. I never used to be like this but I can't help it.

And so now, if I am looking for a card, I always try to find one that I think you would have chosen. I still want to send cards from both of us, even though it's only my name inside, so I choose those with butterflies or fairies on, so that you can carry the message too.

*****

I called in at the sandwich place on the way home from town. I fancied a brie and cranberry baguette and a Kit Kat and I knew from experience that they did a good job there.

'Would you like salad with that?' the woman asked, looking as though she was gutting a fish as she split the submarine roll lengthways.

'No thank you,' I replied.

Filling time as well as the baguette, the woman struck up conversation.

'Been shopping, then?'

The carrier bags probably gave me away.

'What's it like?' she went on. 'Busy?'

'No, it's not too bad actually. It's cold, though.'

'I know,' she said, 'I thought that when I came in this morning.'

I wasn't a regular customer, but I had occasionally been in for something to eat and I knew the woman by sight. She recognised me too, but neither of us knew the other's name.

'You used to push a lady in a wheelchair, didn't you?' she asked. 'I used to see you coming up the road. My house faces straight down the street.'

'Yes,' I replied. 'Yes, I did.'

'Was it your wife? I haven't seen you with her for a long time.'

I nodded slightly. 'She died,' I said.

Pausing only briefly, I realised that I had shocked both of us into silence. I had to break it.

'She had cancer,' I continued, 'she died in September.'

'I'm sorry to hear that. I used to see you together a lot. How are you managing?'

Without droning on or breaking down in tears, I was able to hold a conversation about you and how hard you had fought. It was, strangely, comforting to be able to talk so openly about the situation. It was helpful to me to face up to the facts. And our frank exchange meant that I would be able to talk to the woman again, should I meet her.

As I walked out with my lunch, I realised I still didn't know her name.

*****

During the past few months I have been writing a book about you; about us. *Bright Lights and Fairy Dust* is my working title. The diaries and journals I kept amounted to several thick exercise books and I want to tell your story. I am sure it will be helpful to people who have been affected by cancer, helpful to carers, professionals and to those who, like me, have been bereaved by the disease. I want to tell the story of what you and those around you experienced after your diagnosis. This writing has become my mission. People tell me it is – must be – cathartic. Until today I didn't know the meaning of the word but, now that I do, I can appreciate that I am drawing strength from putting into words some of the things that happened during your illness. Now, there's a thing. Is that what was wrong? You had an illness?

Illness affects us all from time to time, but yours was always going to end in death.

*****

I got that feeling, again, that my life is over too. I couldn't snap out of my gloom this morning and I just kept wondering if my life would ever be happy again. It's not that I'm not supported by my family and friends. They are fantastic and do everything they can to help me on my journey through grief. It's that your passing has left me so, so empty that it cannot be reconciled in my mind. Perhaps the analysts would say that this is the 'denial' phase of grief.

*****

Your last months with us were intense. I was emotionally charged and you were riddled with pain. The strange thought came to me today that because I was with you almost constantly, I lived your cancer too. But, of course, instead of dying with you I am now left here.

I try to recall our happy time together – and God knows we had twenty-four wonderful years and a rock solid marriage – but I keep returning to the dark days of your cancer, when you were confined to bed because of pain. The moment of your death often comes to me, too, and then, sometimes, the image of you in the Chapel of Rest.

Such memories come and go without warning. I know that I cannot stop them and they are part of what we had, but I do think sometimes that to exchange a dark memory for a bright one would be nice.

If I had gone with you I could never have told your story, but I often find myself saying out loud, 'Just let me finish your book, Darling, then you can come for me.'

I fear that my wounded heart may never heal, although I hope it will. I love and miss you so much.

Five Months

My pain is nothing compared to the pain and torment you suffered, but oh, my heart aches for you.

I love and miss you, my Darling, more than anyone could know.

As I tap out *Bright Lights and Fairy Dust* on the computer, I know that I am writing your story to be recorded in perpetuity and that it will live on long after I leave this place to be with you. And I'll say it again, as much as I am recounting the beautiful days, I recall the dark days, too. I pine for you. I miss your touch, your voice, your very presence. I never imagined that it would be like this. In fact I never imagined what it would be like, but I miss you with all the passion with which I love you.

*****

Sara has been having a hard time with the pregnancy. After years of trying and then two attempts with IUI, she and Wayne were referred for IVF and at last, several weeks ago, they learned that it had been successful.

However, Sara has been producing too much fluid. She is breathless, swollen and uncomfortable. I sent her a text:

Oh, darling, how I wish you would not suffer like this, but I hope all is unfolding as it should. Thinking of you constantly, x
Daddy Chris. x

She replied with a text:

The pain I am in now will just make the end result that much more precious. As soon as I feel better I am going to sleep for a week! You would be so proud of your little boy. He has cared for me so well. I love him so much!

*****

My Dad had an appointment with the Consultant Dermatologist about his leg. He'd been referred because he has developed some serious swelling and discolouration below the knees. Vasculitis was the term used to describe his legs. I advised him (and Mum) to be sure to tell the consultant that Dad is often tired and has joint pains. Dad has been telling me this for a few weeks.

At the hospital, the consultant checked Dad's legs and considered all the other symptoms. He then arranged for a range of blood tests and a biopsy.

When Mum and Dad got home, Dad read out over the phone to me what had been written on the blood test cards.

I did a bit of work on the internet and it appeared to me that the consultant might be thinking there's a problem with Dad's autoimmune system, and I'll tell you why, Darling. Firstly, one of the blood tests listed was for 'C3 and C4'. These are particular proteins, called 'complement' proteins (hence the 'C') which work with the body's immune system. High levels of these can be seen in cancer, whilst low levels may suggest problems with the kidneys, liver and heart, and with lupus. Another test, for ANA (AntiNuclear Antibodies) also helps with diagnosis of autoimmune disease. A positive result may come from someone with cancer or lung disease, but can also be found in persons of an elderly nature or those with a history of rheumatic disease (like Dad).

However, I kept coming back to lupus. Perhaps, because he's on so much medication, Dad has 'DILE' – 'Drug Induced Lupus Erythematosus' or, Heaven forbid, perhaps he has what I dread the most, but have told him honestly, that thing called 'cancer'.

He had a core biopsy a few days later. We have to wait now for the results.

*****

I buried your nephew David today, two years to the day since his death. Rather, I interred his ashes in the place he loved so much: the grounds at the back of his flat. The time had come, I thought. He couldn't stay on the shelf – quite literally – indefinitely, and so I set off north with digging tools and a small, twelve inch square concrete slab. When I got there I dug a neat hole as deep as the area around the old Anderson shelter would allow and prepared it to take the container, which I had wrapped in a thick, polythene bag.

In the presence of his friends and neighbours I laid David to rest. I had no fancy words to say and, although I'd considered it, I didn't offer a prayer out loud either, just the phrase, 'David, may you rest in peace'. I laid a piece of broken quarry tile over the top of the container, backfilled the area around it with most of the soil I'd taken out, then capped it with the concrete slab, which I made sure was level with the surrounding grass so that the lawn mower man would be able to whizz clean over it.

*****

I've made all the arrangements for my trip to the States now, Darling. My new passport has come through, I've got my ESTA (Visa Waiver Program) and I have spoken to Deirdre, Carl and Hermione and worked out an itinerary that fits in with them. I will be flying with British Airways.

I'm excited, but also a little nervous as I'm travelling alone. And I'm going to travel light for the first time. If I can't fit it into my backpack, it stays here.

*****

You received a letter today, from the chairman of a well known retail chain. The letter was bursting with enthusiasm and good news.

'Dear Mrs Page,' it began. *'Breathe in the new air.'*
If only.

Further enticement followed. They were holding an event.

'Do try to make Sunday.'
That would be something, wouldn't it?

But the letter still didn't end there. Oh no! Words of encouragement concluded the text:

'Be lucky and happy.'

I would have to calm myself before constructing a reply, but I would definitely write a letter back. I cannot be the only one in my situation to receive such mail and my heart goes out to everyone who has ever been affronted in this way. '*Cold calling*', albeit by letter, seems to be an appropriate name for this type of correspondence.

*****

I was working on *Bright Lights and Fairy Dust*, having made an early start, when the house phone rang. It was Saturday morning and I ignored the call because I was trying to finish the piece I was working on before flying to the US. My trip is less than one week away. The house phone stopped ringing, but my mobile phone kicked in immediately afterwards. Mum's number came up on the screen, so I answered it. At that moment I think I'd worked out that the call I had just ignored had also been Mum.

'Where are you?' she asked.

'At home,' I replied. She must have thought that odd, having just rung the house and got no reply.

'Can you come up?' she continued.

'No problem. I'm on the way.'

I threw a few bits together, grabbed a tenner and my glasses, and raced out of the house like an ambulance man on a shout. Ignoring the speed limits, I drove as quickly as I could to my parents' house. I didn't bother to reverse up their drive. Something was wrong. I had sensed it in Mum's voice.

The front door was open, so I went straight into the hall.

'I'm up here, Chris,' Mum called out, still with that same quiver in her voice.

I went upstairs and into their bedroom, to find Mum mopping Dad's forehead with a damp flannel and Dad a poor colour, making incomprehensible sounds and then apparently 'drifting away'. His eyes rolled backwards, his neck distended, his colour changed from pale to very flushed. His breathing became noisy and he seemed to lose consciousness. I thought he was having a mini-stroke – a TIA (a transient ischaemic attack).

'This is bad, Pa,' I said, as he came round.

'I know, Son,' he managed to mumble.

'That's the sixth one he's had now.' Mum was worried.

So was I.

'I don't know what's wrong,' I said, 'but I think you're going to have to go to hospital.' I took Dad's hand and, as he tried to grip me, held it to my lips and wept. My Dad was not only dying, but he was dying right there in front of me. How cruel, I thought, that I had watched your sister, Brenda, die, then her son, David, then you, my Darling Linda. And now I had to witness the passing of my father.

'The thing is,' I started to explain to them both, 'I could call an ambulance – dial 999 – but they'd just pack you off to A&E and Dad might be stuck on a trolley for hours. I'd rather a doctor came to the house.'

Between us, Mum and I made sure Dad wasn't left alone for a second. He had another 'episode' and just before he lost consciousness again he muttered, in muffled tones, 'Here it comes again.' The same signs presented. As he came back, I asked him if he had any pain.

'No,' he replied.

Using the phone in the hall, I called the out of hours doctor service. I described Dad's signs and told the dispatcher that I would like a doctor to come to the house.

'That's twelve now,' Mum called down to me.

The dispatcher arranged for a doctor to call me on the house phone. When he rang I suggested that Dad might be having a series of TIAs. The doctor said he would get someone to come out, but also told me to dial 999 if his condition worsened.

I went back upstairs and, among the three of us, we spent one of the longest half-hours of our lives as Dad continued to have the 'episodes'. It was awful to watch. He knew when an attack was coming, said he could feel it coming on. His eyes rolled backwards, his colour turned almost to crimson, his hands started to shake and his breathing was heavy and laboured. As he came out of an episode his colour drained completely and he was then drenched with sweat. I couldn't get a pulse, but that didn't surprise me because of Dad's atrial fibrillation.

I called the out of hours doctor service again. If the doctor was going to be much longer I felt I would have to call for an ambulance because Dad kept on having the episodes. The dispatcher told me the doctor was just finishing his current call and that Dad's was next on his list.

Another half-hour passed before the doctor arrived. From the bedroom window I watched the Land Rover back onto the drive then I went downstairs to let the doctor in. It was Dr. Sandhu, the same doctor who attended our house on the weekend you died and who pronounced your death. And yet, right then, I felt a sense of relief, as though you had made sure that the right man was going to take care of Dad. The rational side of me told me that it was just coincidence that Dr. Sandhu had arrived. However, because lately I am receptive to the idea that there might be a parallel plane, I thought that you had been watching Dad's gradual decline over a long period. I thought that you, having witnessed a succession of doctors failing to establish the reasons and prescribing a concoction of medication to get him through, were now positioned to help him from wherever you are. I'll never know, but you may even have helped me to take the decision that I did – to call a doctor and not an ambulance. Whatever was going on, I had complete faith now in Dr. Sandhu, that he would do the right thing for Dad.

Mum and I tried to give Dr. Sandhu Dad's medical history and the latest changes to his health (the vasculitis). While the doctor was checking Dad's blood pressure and pulse, Dad started to have yet another episode, his twenty-first in an hour and a half.

'I don't think your Dad's having mini strokes, Chris', Dr. Sandhu suggested. 'I think he's having seizures.'

'Like little fits, you mean?' I asked.

'Exactly that.'

The doctor arranged for ambulance transport and it wasn't long before an ambulance arrived at the house, closely followed by a paramedic in his rapid response car. With urgency, the medical team now in attendance worked to get Dad out of the house and into the ambulance. I had already moved some furniture because I knew he would have to go to in to hospital, so the way out was as clear as I could make it for them.

The ambulance crew loaded Dad into the ambulance and the paramedic set up an ECG, which Dr. Sandhu examined. As a result of what he saw on the heart trace he revised his instructions and instead of admitting Dad by way of the Clinical Decision Unit – which was almost certainly going to be an improvement on going through Accident and Emergency – he changed it to the Coronary Care Unit. The ambulance raced off on blue lights. The paramedic travelled in the ambulance, leaving his car outside the house, and Mum sat beside Dad all the way. She told me later that it was a fast ride and that the crew were worried about Dad's condition.

After the ambulance had left the house, Dr. Sandhu explained his thinking. He told me he initially thought Dad's vasculitis had spread to his brain, because that can cause fitting. He explained that fits come about because there's a problem either with the brain or the heart. He had even thought, as I had, that there might have been a bleed going on in the brain, but, he said, when he saw the ECG trace he changed his mind and reckoned Dad had heart block. This is where the heart no longer 'fires off' on its own. As you know only too well, Linda, the heart is the only muscle in the body with its own built-in stimulator, the sino-atrial or 'SA' node. It's this that fires off a little electrical impulse that makes the heart contract. When it contracts, it pumps and sends oxygenated blood round the body and deoxygenated blood into the lungs to be oxygenated, refreshed. If Dad's SA node wasn't firing properly then his heart wasn't pumping efficiently and in turn that would deprive his brain of fresh, oxygenated blood. Dr. Sandhu told me that Dad's pulse was low and irregular – at one point down to 29 beats per minute.

60 – 80 beats are considered normal, so Dad was only just ticking over. The episodes were likely to have been occurring when his heart had stopped for a bit.

Sending Dad to the CCU was absolutely the right thing to do, because the staff got straight on to him and sorted him out. Dad can remember the ambulance crew and others hitting his chest and saying words to the effect of *'Come on, we can't lose him now'*. At one point, although he only knows this because the staff told him afterwards, he went into asystole and was a flat-liner.

The CCU immediately took Dad into their lab – their theatre area – where they inserted a temporary pacemaker into his heart by way of his groin. The pacemaker took over from his SA node, doubled his pulse to 60, and saved his life.

*****

I feel bad today because I shared a kiss with a girl last night. It wasn't that it was a bad kiss. On the contrary, I enjoyed it, but even as I was taking pleasure in the moment I felt that what I was doing was wrong. Therefore, more correctly, I feel shame today, because it has only been six months since you and I were parted and yet last night I held another woman in my arms. She made me feel masculine and alive again – something I have been missing.

I don't even know how our peck on the cheek, which was intended merely as a goodnight kiss at the end of a party, turned into such a smacker and ended up as a consenting mutual interchange of orbicularis oris and glossi, but it did. She and her friend offered me a lift home, but I declined and said I would walk. I don't think my response was well received, but I felt awkward about what had happened and insisted on walking. On the way home I sent a text: *I'm sorry*, it read, *can I call you tomorrow to explain?*

It was a very small hour when I eventually got home. As I walked into the kitchen my mobile rang and I knew at once who it was. We had a long conversation. I told her I'd enjoyed our kiss very much, but that I felt it was wrong. I didn't dismiss the event though, because I had felt something. She'd enjoyed it, too, she said, and she wanted me, now. Oh, blimey, I began to feel that I had got myself into a bit of a corner. Kissing was one thing, but this was leading on to something else – something I didn't think I wanted. Why, I thought, hadn't I just kissed her on the cheek and left? Our conversation once again gave me a warm feeling below my beltline and I admitted that if I had accepted the offer of a lift she and I would now be in bed together. She knew that, too, and said she respected me for not getting in the car. The thought of sex excited me and it would have been a fantastic release, but I was sure that we would both regret it in the morning. She told me she wanted to get a cab and come straight over. I suggested that we should each go to bed alone and after a few attempts I was eventually successful in saying goodbye and closing the call. Moments later, as I was getting ready for bed, a text appeared on my mobile: *I want to see you, tomorrow*.

*****

The next day, as soon as I woke, the kiss was the first thing on my mind. I was also worried about the text I had received. What if she came over? What would I say to her? How could I reiterate my feelings without upsetting hers?

I drove to Acorn Ridge. As I stood beside your plot I told you what had happened and said I hoped you could forgive my behaviour.

'Oh, Darling,' I said, softly. 'I'm so sorry. I've let you down and now I don't know what to do. Can you help me?'

I took my Mum and sister to the hospital to see Dad. He wasn't good. The CCU had attempted to replace the temporary pacemaker with a permanent one. This should have been a routine surgical procedure, during which leads, or wires, were to be introduced into Dad's heart from an area of his chest just below his left collar bone.

It hadn't gone well. Dad was in theatre for three and a half hours, conscious, in pain, and the person carrying out the procedure could only get one wire in. Two were required.

Dad argued with the doctor and was returned to the unit half done.

'I don't want that bastard coming anywhere near me,' Dad told us. Although he was unwell, he still had some fight left in him.

After dropping Mum and Linda back at home, I prepared myself for what I thought was going to be an awkward telephone exchange with Danielle, the woman I had kissed. I sat in the car and called her number on my mobile. My heart was racing. How was I going to sort this out without hurting her feelings?

We exchanged polite greetings, but I wanted to get straight to the point.

'Where are we after last night's kiss, Danielle? I'm really sorry.'

'Oh, I'm not. But it's okay, Chris. Don't worry. We'd both had a bit to drink. Let's just leave it at that.'

She had set me free.

Thank you, Linda.

*****

I wrote my letter today, my response to the chairman of that well-known retail chain.

Dear...

I am writing to express my extreme displeasure at having just received some promotional mail from, and signed by, you.

As a result of a typo in my wife's details that was perpetuated over many years with another company offering various promotions, I know that her information has been shared and that you now have it on your records.

It has taken me as many as three attempts to get the other company to stop sending promotional literature. I was promised that my wife's details would be removed from the system and, as it has been a while since anything has dropped through the letterbox from the other company, I was feeling much more optimistic that my last communication with them had been successful. That was until your brochure and vouchers arrived.

My wife died six months ago. She never shopped in your stores and whilst I appreciate that you cannot have known of her passing I at least expect, when information has been 'shared', that updates to such information are similarly performed.

Please remove my wife from your mailing list and please ensure you do not replace her details with mine.

I thought it looked okay and so, remembering that 'formal' letters should be signed 'faithfully', signed it as such and popped it in the post.

*****

Because Dad didn't seem to be getting better, I thought I should cancel my trip to the US. He still had the temporary pacemaker wire going up through his groin and into his heart, and now half of the permanent pacemaker. When we visited him in hospital today, he was breathless and clearly anxious about having to go through the procedure again. He told Mum and me that the staff had never seen so much blood from a pacemaker insertion.

He also told me that I wasn't to cancel my trip.

*****

Dad was left alone by the medical team yesterday. The procedure to fit the second wire was put off, perhaps because he had been so wound up about it. However, he was taken back to the theatre today because it had to be done if he was ever going to sit up again. The wire in his groin meant that he had to lay almost flat and that couldn't continue.

Mum reported back to me later in the evening that, under sedation, Dad's second wire had gone in at last, although once again it had taken longer than usual. The problem, apparently, had been his artificial heart valve. She said that on the way back to the CCU, he could be heard swearing, even using the f-word. He was definitely on the mend.

Eventually the temporary wire was withdrawn and he was moved from CCU into one of the side wards. This was another positive step.

That evening, I packed my single item of baggage – my carry-on backpack – and set my mind for the adventure ahead of me. I turned in just before midnight, knowing that the next day was going to be a long one.

America 1

My first visit to the US without you, Linda, was a massive step for me to take.

Dark imaginings had entered my mind as I counted down to the start of my two week break. Friends had calmed my fears a while ago by saying, simply and with encouragement, 'But they speak English, Chris. It's not as if there's a language barrier. You'll be fine.'

British Airways staff had been striking in the run up to my flight, and I didn't know if I would even get off the ground. However, their industrial action finished before I was due to leave.

I was travelling light – lighter than ever before – and I had also swapped my metal rings and belly bar for plastic so as not to cause a problem at the airport. I got the RailAir coach from Reading to Heathrow with time in hand.

When I checked in online yesterday, I was pleased to have got a seat near one of the exits. When I boarded today, I sat next to a woman who told me, as we swapped polite exchanges, that she was from New Hampshire and was returning to the US after attending a surprise birthday party in the UK. We introduced ourselves. Her name was Sheridan.

When the *fasten seat belt* light came on and the plane started its descent towards her home territory,

Sheridan and I became engaged in deeper conversation. Throughout the flight she had been making notes on what I thought might be a college project, but now Sheridan told me she was editing a book for a friend. I told her I was writing a book myself, and I hoped I would eventually get to a point where my own manuscript would need editing.

As we made our final approach into Boston Logan, I explained that you had died and that I was writing your story, the story of our journey through your cancer. I said that you and I had both felt that we had gone through a portal as the disease progressed and had been given sight of, and access to, something 'spiritual'. Describing what I meant wasn't easy, but then Sheridan told me that the book her friend had written was all about spiritualism. We both then bristled with enthusiasm and couldn't stop talking about spiritualism, or you, even after we had touched down and taxied to the terminal.

I recommended a book to her that The Enchanted Manor had given us. Do you remember? *'Messages From Nature's Guardians',* by Fiona Murray, is about the Fairies and Elementals that surround us and look after us.

Sheridan said she would pass on the information to her friend. Then she wrote down her friend's email address in the back of my journal and I told her I would drop her friend a note about my book, on my return to the UK. Sheridan was also interested in the story I had to tell, so she added her own email address too.

I had no hold baggage and went straight to the Customs and Border Patrol officer with my backpack and the little white carrier bag that had travelled with me from Heathrow. I was photographed and fingerprinted and, after being quizzed about the luscious contents of the carrier bag, was told to enjoy my stay and my candy. Making my way towards the exit, I saw Sheridan again and managed to say goodbye to her one last time before she disappeared into the Massachusetts crowd.

Despite all my concerns about my trip, I had done quite a bit of preparation for it back at home, using the internet. You'd be impressed, Darling! I identified certain things that I felt I *must* do and others that would be *nice* to fit in.

The first experience on my list was a water taxi across the bay, from the airport to the Aquarium. The free bus from the airport set me down at the boat dock terminal but there was no one there. I suddenly felt vulnerable and had no idea how long I would have to wait for the next boat. It was cold and the sky was dull. My destination was just across the water, but it might as well have been back across the Atlantic. Eventually, a boat drew alongside. By now, one other passenger was waiting and we cast off into the green waters of Massachusetts Bay. As the boat bobbed across the bay, I was afforded my first close-up views of Boston.

My hotel was already booked: The Harborside Inn, a short walk from the Aquarium.

As well as spending a few days in Boston, I had lots of 'New' things planned. Deirdre and Leroy were in New Hampshire, Carl and Fran in New York and Roger and Hermione in New Jersey. These were important visits that I wanted to make on your behalf – in your memory – and I found it very sad that we couldn't be together for this adventure.

After checking into the hotel, I asked where I could find the nearest pharmacy. At the very least I needed razor blades, toothpaste and mouthwash, things I was unlikely to have been allowed to carry with me on the plane. The local equivalent to our Boots was a CVS and while I was walking there I saw 'The Living Room', an American restaurant on Atlantic Avenue. The menu looked good and I knew right away that I would pop back after shopping.

It didn't disappoint and I was made to feel welcome. The service and the food were excellent and, to my surprise, I wasn't at all awkward with my own company. I would definitely be going back there, I thought.

I had hoped for a good first night's rest after my long day, made even longer, of course, by the time difference, but something was going on in the street below and my sleep was disturbed until the small hours. There was loud shouting, but I couldn't decide if it was fighting or just boisterous enthusiasm among the voices.

*****

My mobile phone – *your* mobile phone actually, which was on Pay As You Talk – worked for only a short time before running out of credit. This was unexpected enough, but my situation was made worse because I didn't know your PIN number. Vodafone wouldn't give it to me for data protection reasons and the hotel wouldn't permit me to make a call on any of their landlines. And this was only my second day! I resorted to e-mailing Wayne from a computer terminal in the lobby, hoping that he could purchase some credit back home and pass me the twelve digit voucher number.

Wayne and Sara were, of course, five hours ahead of me, and when I got back from my meal at The Living Room they were almost certainly in bed and asleep, but I logged on anyway. To my delight, Wayne had replied, saying he would get a voucher in the morning. It was something of a miracle that he had even seen my mail, because he had already changed to a different address and was in the process of abandoning the one to which I had sent my SOS. The fleeting thought entered my head that you might have been at work here. Then I went on up to bed, with my hotel earplugs installed to 'muffle the kerfuffle' that I had endured the night before.

*****

As soon as I got up the next morning I went downstairs to log on to the internet again. It was as if Santa had paid me a visit whilst I had slept. It was lunchtime back home. Wayne had purchased a voucher and I was back in communication. I replied immediately and, as well as thanking him for bailing me out, I related my experience of the city so far:

> *Boston has been extremely interesting. I'm always fascinated by ships and yesterday I walked around Charlestown, Bunker Hill and North End to The Boston Naval Yard, where I visited the USS Constitution and the USS Cassin Young. The tour guide told visitors that the Constitution is the oldest ship afloat, making the point that our HMS Victory, although older by more than thirty years, is in dry dock. I enjoyed my visit very much.*

*More walking today, as I head off to Back Bay
and Newbury Street before turning back to South
Station this afternoon. Then I'm heading north to
see Deirdre and Leroy.*
*I hope you're both okay and that Sara's feeling a
little less breathless - and sleeping better.*
*I'll be checking out in about an hour and a half,
so I will lose this internet connection, but I am
very glad it was available!*

*****

Wayne replied a little later, explaining that Sara was
still breathless and her energy levels were low. He was
doing all he could to keep her comfortable.

In his email, although I didn't need reminding, he
also told me how cold Boston was this side of Easter.

I had only a short time there, but I enjoyed the
experience. At the risk of boring you, Darling, I just
want to let you know about some of the other things I
did as well as visiting the Naval Yard.

Just up the road from The Harborside Inn is the Old
State House. This lovely brick and timber building –
surrounded now by high rise buildings – used to be the
seat of colonial government and is now a museum. I
couldn't leave town without taking a peek inside, not
least for the architecture alone, but one of the first
things I had to do, before I was allowed to wander
around the museum, was hand over my backpack and
white carrier bag to the man at the reception desk.

'Oh, my gosh!' he gasped upon seeing the contents
of the carrier bag. 'Are they Maltesers? Where did you
get those? And what else have you got in there? Oooh!'

I was reminded of my offers to Deirdre and to Carl to bring something from England that they can't get in the States and explained the journey the little honeycomb treats and the box of Bassett's had made so far and where they were heading.

'They might not make it,' the staff member joked.

Pleased to have left the Old State House with all with which I had entered, I continued on foot to Boston Common. The imposing building that I saw there, with the gilded dome, is the New State House. Although I didn't go in, I was again impressed by the architecture. But my pleasure didn't end there, because I walked around the outside of the Common and into Beacon Street, where I saw the beautiful brownstone houses of Back Bay, with their bay windows and stone stairs leading from the sidewalks to the front doors, just as you and I have seen in films. I also walked part of Newbury Street. It had to be done! Then I continued on my way. I reached the Bus Terminal at South Station by way of Chinatown and the Chinatown Gate. Everything felt a world away from what I have ever known. I felt as though I was in a film myself.

I think you would have enjoyed Boston.

Well, perhaps not the ships.

Later that evening, Wayne sent a text message to say he'd spoken to my Mum. She said Dad was now on a ward and up and walking about. Dad was sore, but on the mend.

Wayne also passed me details of the latest top-up voucher. Your phone was gobbling them up so quickly! If all this sounds a bit extreme I should point out that the reason it was so important that there was credit on your mobile was because I was going to have to use it to contact Deirdre in New Hampshire and Carl in New York. It wasn't just a case of being 'nice to have', it was essential to my survival.

Wayne replied one more time and as well as buoying me up with more credit, he passed on the excellent news that Dad was going home from hospital.

My bus ride north took about an hour and a half on Interstate 95, a smooth multi-lane highway that made our motorways back home look tired and dated. Deirdre and Leroy met me at the bus station in Portsmouth. And yes, there's a naval base there, too! I haven't seen Deirdre in I don't know how long – since she worked with you at the hospital I suppose, and that must be twenty years ago – but I recognised her at once. I didn't know Leroy, but you used to write to them and you stayed in touch. I was made to feel very welcome.

Just a month before, a powerful storm, called a nor'easter, had pounded the North Eastern States. Although the weather had settled down now, there was evidence of storm damage as we drove to Deirdre and Leroy's home in Newmarket. It was still cold.

I was in New Hampshire now. Once again, I couldn't help thinking about you and how you would have loved seeing your friends in their own lovely home out there in the woods.

From my carrier bag, at last and after a journey of three thousand miles, I pulled out the treat that I had brought for them. The Maltesers were a hit and my baggage was now just a little lighter.

The next day we went for a drive. Deirdre and Leroy wanted to show me something of their countryside. As we drove north into Maine (yes, another state, Doll) I saw a sign for *Kennebunkport* and I asked Deirdre and Leroy if that was where the president stayed. I think I must have heard the name of the place on television at some point, along with a reference to the president. Leroy drove all the way there, to Walker's Point, and we could see the security fencing.

I was only half right, however. It's called the *Bush Compound* and is owned by George Bush Senior, the former president.

It's also guarded by the Secret Service so, unfortunately, there was no going in.

Don't laugh Darling, but back at home, on the internet when I was looking for travel arrangements, I found *Linda Street*. On the map, it's next to the train station at Exeter, about fifteen minutes from Newmarket. My hosts drove me to the station and all I wanted to do was take a snap of the road sign. We must have been right there, on Linda Street, but there wasn't a sign anywhere that confirmed that place on the map. Once again, as I searched for you, I was thwarted and I wonder if that's how it's meant to be. You're there, on Linda Street; I'm here, on Earth.

I should have understood, from the very name, what a Gummy Bear is. But I had to ask. This was when Deirdre's granddaughter was with us in a candy store. When it was explained to me, I realised I had something similar (but not as long-lasting) left in the carrier bag.

After my few days with Deirdre and Leroy I returned to Boston and caught the Acela Express to New York. This was something else I had researched before coming: a train ride of around four hours. It took me south and I looked out over a much waterlogged landscape due, I'm sure, to the earlier storms. We travelled into Rhode Island (yes, Darling, that's another one) and stopped at Providence. Rhode Island is the smallest state, less than fifty miles from North to South, and the train was soon into – wait for it – another state. Most of the remaining journey was through Connecticut and despite the dull weather I remained fascinated by the countryside, the landscape and the architecture.

When I emerged from the depths of Pennsylvania Station, it was dark and raining heavily. My hotel, again one that I had booked back home, was a few blocks away and I chose to walk. When I got to reception, I was dripping wet and after another long day of travelling all I wanted was to dry off and relax. I had arranged just one full day in the city, tomorrow, because Carl was meeting me after work.

*****

It's such a pity that the weather has been dismal. Today was heavy with cloud and rain was forecast. However, I had another ship to visit and having come this far to see it, I wasn't about to give up. I made my way over to Pier 86 on the Hudson River. Security was tight and I, along with all the other visitors, was patted down and told to remove my shoes and everything metal. As I passed through the security scanner I was glad I'd switched my body jewellery to plastic.

When I stepped out on to the pier on which the USS Intrepid Air, Sea and Space Museum is located, there was a bonus for me. On the other side of the pier was the submarine USS Growler. It was only opened to the public last year. I took a self-guided tour of it, taking in the details of its construction and history.

The weather closed in and it rained – hard – but I carried on with my visit. After the submarine, I investigated the Concorde on the pier and was surprised at how small that was. After walking the length of the cabin I sheltered beneath its delta wings and was in awe that this feat of engineering could cross the Altantic in three hours.

For me, though, the main attraction was always going to be the USS Intrepid. This massive aircraft carrier was built during WWII and saw service in the Pacific, but during the 1960s it was the recovery ship for the Mercury and Gemini space missions, all so interesting to me.

There were many planes and helicopters on static display on the flight deck and, like the ship itself, these aircraft were museum pieces. As a schoolboy, I had assembled plastic model kits of some of them, so they had my instant attention. But one in particular stood out for me. The Blackbird. Actually, the aircraft on show was the Lockheed A-12, which evolved into the Blackbird. For a plane that was developed in the 1960s, even today it looked like something out of science fiction. I remembered seeing one of these in flight at one of the air tattoos at RAF Greenham Common back in the eighties, and although the aircraft is no longer in service, its design and capabilities are quite simply astonishing.

Eventually, I joined the other visitors inside the ship and began my private tour of Intrepid at my own pace. It was to take me a further four hours, as there was so much to discover. All the while, the weather outside was appalling and, when I looked out from the control tower towards the city, I couldn't see the tops of the skyscrapers.

My meeting with Carl was still a few hours away, so I made my way back into the city and sought shelter from the incessant rain by visiting the New York Public Library. This turned out to be another unexpected bonus. As I wandered around the main foyer, marvelling at the building work, a proud New Yorker asked me if I had been upstairs. 'Look at the ceilings', he said.

They are awesome, Darling. You and I came here in 2000, but we never went inside. I am sure you would be getting the same buzz from all this.

But, again, perhaps not the ships!

I returned to the bar next to my hotel, where I had arranged to meet Carl. We were both on time and in fact spotted one another as we headed for the door. He seemed not to have changed a bit since our last meeting. That was many years ago, when you and I went to Carl and Fran's UK wedding in Newtown.

We sat on stools at the bar and our conversation felt like we were carrying on from only the day before, not years earlier.

It was late when we arrived at Carl and Fran's house on Long Island. The three of us talked for hours, catching up on news and events on both sides of the Atlantic.

'Oh,' I said, 'I almost forgot.' I reached into my bag. 'I brought your Jelly Babies.'

Darling, they don't call it Long Island for nothing. It's 118 miles from one end to the other and although Carl and Fran are at the New York end, they drove east for some retail. We didn't reach the far end of the island, but we called in to several places that back home we call 'Charity Shops', but they call 'Thrift Stores'. I had a great time rummaging around with my bargain-hunting friends and wished I could have had more time there, but I only stayed with them for two nights.

The next morning I went back to Manhattan with Carl as he drove to work, a hot cup of coffee from Fran in his cup holder. We parted company at the Subway and I got the E Train to Penn Station. From there, my next stop was your sister and brother-in-law's in Middletown.

New Jersey had also been affected by recent storms and I wasn't long into my walk from the train station to Roger and Hermione's, when I managed to step in a muddy puddle. You know how immaculate their home is, so you can imagine their reaction when they saw what I had deposited on the kitchen floor. Immediately, before I had even said a proper 'Hello', Roger got the Shark out and erased my recklessness.

I hadn't meant to wreak such mayhem and was careful to take my shoes off after that. As always, though, I was made to feel very welcome and we spent lots of time together catching up on one another's news.

I am sad for you Linda that you can't be here with us; that you couldn't come out on this mini adventure. I'm sure we would all have had a ball.

*****

Well, Darling, this visit to America has really brought out the wanderer in me. That's a first for me on this side of the Atlantic. It's early April and I decided to walk to Red Bank today, to look around the boutiques and shops.

It wasn't a pedestrian-friendly walk and I had to cross the busy highway several times, back and forth, to use a sidewalk. Often there wasn't one at all and like a tightrope walker I took to toeing my way along the kerb stones, keen not to attract the sound of an angry driver's car horn or shouts of 'keep off the grass', as it was all so neat, tidy and green.

When, after more than three miles of difficult walking, I reached the outskirts of Red Bank, I changed my mind about shopping and decided instead to return to the hotel, but by way of a route that would take me through the suburbs. I had my map of Monmouth County with me. There would be no more fighting with the traffic, I thought.

I went off right, walking first under the railroad bridge and then immediately over the low-level road bridge across the river. I was now in the suburbs, and although there was some traffic, it didn't worry me like it had earlier. There was a gentle climb up a hill into a suburb called River Plaza. It was a beautiful morning, the sky wide and blue and the sun shining brightly. I heard the unmistakable sound of a woodpecker in a nearby tree and I saw some beautiful birds.

Some of the houses were breathtaking in their design or location, nestled among tall pines or surrounded by smaller trees that were thick with spring blossom. There were scents in the air such as I cannot ever recall in England and the very soil itself had a wonderful aroma.

I enjoyed my own company. There were no deadlines except dinner with Roger and Hermione at five, and that was a long way off. I could go as fast or as slow as I wanted. I could stop when something caught my eye or I had to check the map but, most of all, I felt that I was experiencing a little of America at ground level. There weren't any tourist attractions in this part of Monmouth County, but the whole thing was a big attraction for me. My bubble burst though, when a chap in a car shouted at me.

'Fuck you, you faggot!'

As he passed me, I thought he slowed down; thought he would turn his car around and come back to shoot me or do something bad to me. He didn't, but at the time there was a flurry of activity within the walls of my chest and it took a while for my heart rate to settle down again.

When I got back to the hotel, it was after noon and I had been out for over four hours. I could hardly believe it, but I had covered eleven miles. That was eleven miles on asphalt and concrete, on a day that just kept getting warmer when I had no water to hydrate myself and wore a fleece that would have kept anyone warm above the Arctic Circle. I had thoroughly enjoyed it though and, just as I had on Long Island, I had a sense of 'getting into America'.

Roger and Hermione were shocked to hear of my travels, but roared with laughter when I told them about the driver who'd shouted at me.

'He probably thought you had a nice tush.' Hermione laughed loudly. 'Seriously, though,' she said, 'nobody walks around here except the Mexicans; the Hispanics. They're usually on foot or bicycle.'

I sat on the front steps, first with Hermione and then with Roger, but with thoughts of you too, my Darling. Last year was a year of 'lasts'. Now I'm in a year of 'firsts' and this is my first Easter without you.

I am surrounded by people and by love, but so often I feel lonely. My world now, without you, is a different place, and sometimes I do struggle.

*****

After my two busy weeks away, my return to the UK was unremarkable except for one thing, and I'm only telling you this because it really annoyed me. You would probably say I got what I deserved. You might be right.

When I got through customs I stepped out into the early morning air with my single piece of carry on. I saw the bus stand on the far side of the car park and, recognising it as the one where I had been dropped off, started walking towards it. The RailAir bus was just coming in, so I broke into a run. The driver let a single passenger off and was just closing the side locker as I got to the door of the bus. But he wouldn't let me on; said it was a set down point only. I was there, for goodness sake, at the door.

'You'll have to go to the bus station. If anyone sees me letting you on here, I'll be in trouble.'

I asked for directions to the bus station then set off in a hurry. I seemed to run and run, through long passages and underground walkways before eventually popping up at the Heathrow Airport Bus Station. I had never seen it before. With my lungs burning and my heart pounding, I watched the same RailAir bus pull on to the stand. The door opened and the driver looked down at me.

'You made it then.' I didn't know if he was congratulating me or laughing at me and had the journey back to Reading train station to think about it.

*****

Sorry Doll, I meant to say that when I spoke to Mum a couple of days ago, she told me Dad's biopsy results had come through and they were okay. The tests revealed that Dad had 'normal dermatitis'. Is that like saying you had 'normal cancer'? Don't get me wrong, I am extremely happy that the test didn't turn up anything more sinister.

Bizarrely, I think that Dad's recent problems and his hospitalisation have saved his life. I also remain convinced that his medication was on the way to killing him.

*****

I had a bit of an awkward moment this morning as I was swapping my plastic body jewellery back to metal after returning from the States. I couldn't get the belly bar back in. And having already taken out the plastic one, I couldn't even get that back in. I remembered the advice I'd been given that it could take a while to heal. Perhaps I had been too hasty. Oh well, when it's settled down (it's a little sore now) I will go back to the tattoo shop and get it done again.

*****

I don't know if you remember Adrian, Darling. He and I worked together for years, so you might have met him. He got married today to Carrie but you definitely won't have met her. They haven't been together long and I have yet to be introduced. Before I went to the States though, they sent me an invitation to their evening celebrations. I wasn't sure if I would be able to go. By that I mean I didn't know if I would be able to handle all the fuss, the people, the conversations. But I decided it was the right thing to do. The venue, a local pub, wasn't familiar to me and I was nervous. As I walked in I felt like a cowboy in one of those western movies, pushing open the saloon doors into the hubbub of the celebrations. Just as I was wondering if I would know anyone, immediately to my left I spotted Adrian dancing with the person I guessed to be his new wife. They were dancing together on a small area of uncarpeted floor, in front of a loud disco; the only ones dancing. I nodded to them and although I'd never met Carrie, she returned a smile. I moved through the bar to the restaurant area where, thankfully, I met other ex-work colleagues. And although we had to raise our voices a little, to counter the music, I was soon in conversation catching up on their news and telling them mine.

In the end, I was pleased I had gone and when I got home I managed to sleep well for a change.

*****

I mentioned I met Sheridan on the plane to Boston. I've been home a few days now and, just as I told Sheridan I would, I sent an email today to her friend, Berenice. I hope she doesn't mind, because we're total strangers.

And I also hope you don't mind.

In my email I explained that I was writing a book about what you went through, battling terminal cancer, and that you died in September. It was because Sheridan was editing Berenice's book about spiritualism that I felt driven to write and tell her how you and I both thought we had been given access to a 'spiritual' world neither of us had seen before. I told her that I still believe there is something out there and what you and I experienced – and what I continue to experience – can't be explained. I wrote that there is magic everywhere I go now. Having sat next to probably the only passenger out of more than three hundred who was editing a book on the spiritual world, I thought, backed up my feelings.

I attached a few pages from *Bright Lights and Fairy Dust*, hoping she might comment. I'm only half way through writing up my notes, but I told Berenice I wanted to get back to work on it as soon as I had sorted myself out after my trip.

I was delighted to get a reply the same day.

Berenice wrote back that she was honoured that I had shared with her what she called our Love Story. She thinks of life, in her words, 'as a constant awakening to one's spirit' and, she put, 'it's through our challenges that we become present to the magic, mystery and miracles that await discovery in our lives'. She wrote that what you and I felt, and in my case continue to experience, is this awakening.

In the book she is writing, she wants to bring a greater understanding of the spirit and consciousness we all share. Berenice believes it is what truly unites us as a global people.

She told me that our story is important; that it is rich and poignant and will offer healing to many, including me.

Wow! I'm not crazy after all. I found her reply uplifting and encouraging. I read it several times to make sure I understood her comments and I knew I could relate to everything she had written. I was also pleased with her positive response to the short extracts of my book.

*****

The next day I received another email from America, this time from Sheridan. She wrote that Berenice had received my note and was happy to hear from me. Sheridan had also read the extracts from *Bright Lights*. 'It is a powerful story', she wrote, and she thanked me for allowing her to read the extracts.

*****

I bought a delicate, life-sized white butterfly, made from a feather and papier mache and hand finished with black edging. It was one of a few nods to you as I prepared for Mikee and Emma's wedding next week. My intention is to have it as my buttonhole. Apart from trousers (and I would need trousers) I was pretty much set as far as what to wear.

*****

It's mid April, Darling, and I just thought you might be interested to know that there has been a second eruption under a glacier at Eyjafjallajökull in Iceland. No, I've never heard of it, either. It erupted for the first time less than a month ago.

Now, today, airports are being closed because of the dangers from the huge amount of volcanic ash in the air that could get sucked into jet engines. Once again,

I realise how lucky I was to have flown to the States and back.

The 'magic' at work?

*****

I was at the Retail Park this afternoon and got so upset that I started crying in a public place. I cried because I felt such sadness for you, my Darling Linda. Yes, I was sad for myself, because I'm here and you're there, but at the Retail Park today I remembered our shopping trips, when we went out in the car and I helped you from the car into the wheelchair. I pushed you wherever you wanted to go. You loved shopping – for anything. Sometimes you would ask me to leave you and, somehow, you managed to get that wheelchair around the shops without my help. You described so many things as 'beautiful', even items in shops, and I wonder with awe, how you managed to do that when you knew you were dying.

And that is what made me so sad today.

That evening I sent Wayne and Sara another email. It was a rant from a grumpy old man who'd had a disastrous day trying to locate some wedding apparel.

Howdy Folks,

I went to buy trousers again today. Not to buy more and more trousers, but still trying to find a pair in a fabric, style, colour and size that works for me. I need a decent pair of trousers for Emma and Mikee's wedding tomorrow. Whenever I have found what I think is the right style, the shop doesn't have my size; or they have my waist size but not a long enough leg. When they do have something close to my size I don't like the pattern, or the hang. Inside leg, to my surprise, can vary by a few inches according to where I find the trousers. In some stores a 'regular' leg is a 32; in others, 31. Both are too short. To find a 'long' is surprise enough, but some 'long' trousers are 33 and some are 34. Too long: they ball up across my shoes and at the bottom of my legs and I feel awkward. On this basis I have to suppose that 32½ is the ideal inside leg and that ought to cover all the store variances, but that isn't an off-the-peg size. I need a seamstress to help me. She would either have to let down the short ones, if there's enough spare fabric below the hem, or else take up the long ones, okay if the legs are straight, but a bind if they're tapered. Jeans. I could wear jeans. But this is a big 'famiglia inglese' wedding; jeans wouldn't be right. Nope, I'm going to have to find some middle ground. I had tried to find some in America, but their trousers, just like the ones here, are made across the globe and I didn't find what I was looking for. Yesterday I tried all the main stores here without success. Today I drew a blank at the Retail Park. But I did find some trousers eventually, at the supermarket of all places. Unfortunately the checkout person wasn't a seamstress.

Love to you,
Pops
xx

*****

The next morning I was still struggling with my wardrobe. I needed your help again.

The trousers I bought from the supermarket yesterday didn't have quite the same attraction for me now. Linda, I'm sure I wouldn't be in this state of mind if you were here with me. You would tell me whether or not they look good. You might even assure me that I'm more important than any clothes (although I still need clothes, of course).

Anyway, I dashed into town early and returned to one of the department stores. I bought jeans. At least, I *think* they're jeans but, because of the colour and the light fabric, and because my options were now seriously limited, in my mind they could probably be described as casual trousers. I'd spotted them two days earlier but passed them over precisely because they looked like jeans and also because they were a bit pricey. I tried on two pairs – a 32 leg and a 34 leg. The 34 was much too long (as in my previous rant to Wayne). I would have to settle for the 32 and just make sure I didn't pull them up under my armpits. I was finally ready for the wedding celebrations.

My mind, however, was not so straight. I thought back to the special hen night Emma had with you and everyone else last year and it made me sad again that you're not here. I know you saw her wedding dress, because Emma had come to the house with photos of her trying it on in the bridal shop and only you were allowed to see them. While sorting out your things – your paperwork – I found the manila envelope that I knew contained those pictures. You had written on it, in bold capital letters, *TOP SECRET KEEP OUT*. So I left it folded over and would wait to see the dress for myself.

The wedding was lovely. It was a beautiful spring afternoon. The sun was shining and it was a clear day; clear of any aircraft, too. No sounds and no vapour trails to scar the sky. That volcano was still keeping planes on the ground. There was a peace all around such as I have never known in my life.

From my place in the church, I aimed my pocket-sized Coolpix at Father and Daughter as the music announced their entrance. If I had managed a reasonable shot I would have been surprised. Emma practically ran up the aisle. She was so, so happy and in no time at all, it seemed to me, she became Mrs. Warren. And yes, her dress was gorgeous.

The congregation followed the bride and groom outside for photographs – lots of photographs. I thought it likely that it would be a while before I was called into a shot, so I went back inside the church and had a quiet moment. I was happy for Mikee and Emma. This was a wedding. It was always going to be a happy day. I cast my mind back to our wedding and felt tears sting the corners of my eyes. We were happy, Darling, and you and Wayne made my life complete. I miss you very much.

But hey! I had to get with it; be strong. I can't change what's happened to us. I dabbed my eyes and stepped back out into the sunshine for family photos.

At the reception, the DJs played every request that had been returned to Mikee and Emma on their invitation replies. When *So Do I* came on I had to hold back tears again, but hearing it brought you back to me. I don't know if it was the song, but I seemed to draw strength and I was able to enjoy the celebrations and the dancing that followed.

*****

I went to the supermarket this afternoon and on the way saw two planes in the sky. I don't even know why I looked up. One of the aeroplanes was very high and the other at a lower altitude and on what appeared to be a very, very wide arc. Both were streaming vapour trails behind them and flying in a vaguely easterly direction. If it sounds odd that I should comment on this, please bear in mind that the United Kingdom still has a 'no fly' airspace above it because of the ash cloud sent up by the erupting volcano named 'Eyjafjallajökull' [pronounced 'Aya-Fiatla-Yukutla'] in Iceland. It's been spewing ash since last Wednesday and all UK flights have been grounded since last Thursday for fear that flying through the dust cloud could cause engines to fail. Who wants to be on board during a flameout?

But who wants to be on board the first wave of aircraft that gets back up there when we're told that it's okay to fly again? Even if those first few planes do get on okay, who's to say the dust won't have attacked their engines or their airframes? Evidently the dust can be highly corrosive. I don't know about you, but my mind's running away with the notion that planes might fall out of the sky months from now if any of that volcanic stuff connects with jet engines. Stay down. Lie low. Wait for the dust to settle and then get back up there.

By the way, inside the supermarket the fruit and vegetable aisles were very thinly stocked and even empty in places. What's to become of us, that we should have to live off UK-grown cabbage and spinach now? This is going to hurt us all, especially if the situation continues. The knock-on effect will be expensive for everyone. And the gas from greens can be painful.

Just what were those planes I saw?

*****

Ever since we first moved to the East Fields, you and I had our black and green wheelie bins at the back of the house. And every week one of us would undo the back gate and tilt and haul one colour or the other down the side of the garage and out to the path at the front.

I've changed that, Darling. I thought it would be easier if the bins were always ready at the front of the house. So I've put them at the side of the garage. It's only four paces now to the path. And it's nothing to take a loaded pedal bin liner to the front door instead of the back.

And okay, when I want to use the green bin, I know I'll have to bring it into the back garden now in order to fill it. But I still think my change makes sense.

*****

After a very quiet week, the noise is back: the noise of aeroplanes. Even when I think they're not about, I only have to cock an ear and I can hear them again. They're everywhere, filling the air with a background rumble. It was only when they weren't flying that I stopped to consider how much a part of our daily lives they are. In all my life they've never been absent because jet engines were put into commercial airliners a few years before I was born. They've always been around. Over the years I have sometimes managed to put distance between them and me. On the other hand, for example when, in the late seventies, I moved first to Slough and then to Maidenhead for a while, I got very close to them. With London Heathrow only a few miles away, it was necessary then, in order for me to function, to blank myself off to their incessant output and it wasn't long before I got used to their noise.

The situation in Iceland has reverted to something close to 'normal' now and the sound of birdsong comes in second again behind air traffic.

*****

I rang the doorbell and took a small step back, turning slightly as I did so to look at the other houses in the little cul-de-sac. It was just after four o'clock and Emma and Mikee had invited the family to a barbeque and garden party. Unfortunately, the weather had changed and there was light rain in the air. I was greeted at the door by Emma and her two dogs, Basil and Blue, who checked me out as I stepped indoors.

'Hello Uncle Chris!' Emma gushed with her usual enthusiasm for everything. She hadn't finished. 'Or, should I say, *Great* Uncle Chris?'

I was caught off guard for a moment. How did she know? I hadn't told anyone that Sara was pregnant. I couldn't think of what to say and my brain buzzed inside my head. Then I realised what she meant.

'You're pregnant?' I asked, trying to turn my obvious shock into the joyous response her news deserved. 'That's fantastic. When is it due?'

'New Year's Day.'

In my mind, even as I asked the question, I hoped that Sara would have her babies before Emma. I know that was a selfish thought, but Wayne and Sara have been trying for years now to have a baby and I think I wanted *you* to have the news before anyone else. After your diagnosis, they wanted to bring such news to you and we all know you would have been overjoyed. But you had to go before they got their wish.

*****

Hello, my Love.

It's the first May Bank Holiday weekend. Today is Sunday and I can see on the calendar that you have been gone from me for exactly seven months.

It's also the day that I am walking the Sarsen Trail. I have been trying to prepare myself these past few weeks for this marathon walk from Avebury to Stonehenge across Salisbury Plain, something I have done a few times now. The weather forecast isn't good, but I'm not going to let that put me off.

The last time I did this was, I think, two years ago. You were scheduled to work that weekend, so I couldn't have use of our car, but through my work I was lucky enough to borrow a BMW. I enjoyed a very fast drive to Stonehenge early on the morning of the big walk.

By the time I started walking from Avebury that day, I knew that you would be up and getting ready to go to work. You might even have made an early start too, I can't remember. I phoned you, to tell you '*I love you*' and that I had started my 26-miler and would update you as I went. You didn't have to know how my walk was doing. I could have waited until I'd finished and then phoned you. But, as with everything I did, you took an interest. You were the first to admit that you couldn't walk the Sarsen Trail, but that didn't stop you from encouraging me.

As that day went on I got into a stride, a pace I thought I could manage comfortably. I found myself covering a mile every twenty minutes, so I began texting you with a mileage countdown. After two hours I had 20 miles left to walk; after four hours 14, and so on. My texts became more frequent as I walked but, just as the miles were knocked off, so my physical situation deteriorated. I had pain in my groin, my leg muscles were on fire, and I developed hotspots in my boots. Walking became very uncomfortable.

At The Bustard on Salisbury Plain, when I went to get my entry card stamped at the marshal's post, my pain must have been obvious. I remember very clearly what the man behind the trestle table said as he signed the card.

'Do you want the St. John's to take you to Stonehenge? You look pretty rough.'

And I remember my reply.

'I've just walked 22 miles,' I said. 'You'd look rough, too. But I haven't walked all this way to give up on the last four.'

I was in agony and every step hurt. My feet, my legs, my back were all complaining. When the 2-mile marker came into view, I sent you another text, but I wasn't counting down the miles anymore; I was counting down the time. Even as I tapped out my messages I was thinking how much longer I had to put up with the pain. My wonderful marathon walk had turned into an endurance test and I knew I was struggling.

When I finally reached Stonehenge I sent you a text to let you know that I had finished. I thought my finishing time was respectable, but by then I could hardly walk without wincing. I used the refreshment voucher I had earned to get a cup of tea and a bag containing a slice of pizza, an apple and some cake. I sat on one of the straw bales and tucked in eagerly. It tasted good. I went to get up to go first to the bin and then to the car. My body wasn't working properly anymore and the messages from my brain to my legs seemed to be delayed, or misinterpreted. As I hobbled back to the BMW, doing my best to make my gait appear normal, I must have looked like a frail, old, man who would have done well to have stayed home that day. That's certainly how I felt.

But you were pleased for me, that I had achieved my goal.

Today's walk was better, although the weather was bad, with wind and rain. It wasn't the same without your support though. With every step I knew I was pushing myself but I had no one to share in my success. My phone was silent.

I still managed about 3 miles an hour and I think I'll do it again next year, but I'll train harder. And hope the rain holds off.

*****

I have travelled all over the place since you died. I have seen friends and family on both sides of the Atlantic and on both sides of the family. Friends of yours; mutual friends; your family; in ways I didn't see them when you were alive – when we would visit together.

And yet I am lonely. Not alone, but lonely. As I have gone from place to place, I have wondered what it is that I am looking for. My whole world is now empty and I rattle around in it, lost, because I can't seem to find anything to grab hold of that makes any sense.

*****

Here we go again, Linda. It's only been two weeks since flights in our area resumed, but some low cost airlines that use smaller airports have announced more cancellations today because that volcano in Iceland is playing up again. It's sending yet more debris up into the atmosphere. Weather forecasters are saying that northerly winds over Britain this weekend could bring the ash back over Ireland and western Scotland.

*****

I sent an e-mail to New York:

Dear Carl and Fran,

I hope you're both well. By now your weather ought to be a whole lot warmer. If it is, please, please send some our way. We're fed up with having to keep the furnace going and having to put an extra blanket on the bed at night. We're only weeks away from the longest day, but I still have to wear a coat when I go out!
Rant over.

Wayne and Sara were finally able to confirm that they are to be parents, after three and a half years of IUI and IVF. I'm gonna be a grand daddy. There's more: they're having twins! They won't be identical, because they're not in the same sac, so it could be one of each sex, or two of the same. Wayne and Sara want to maintain the surprise anyway, so we won't know until November, which is when Sara's due. She's having a tough time of it at the moment and everyone hopes things will improve as time goes on.

They still haven't moved yet. Wayne found a house while Sara was in hospital and sold their flat in the same week, but there is a break in the chain at the far end, so it's holding everything up. That said, the solicitors have suggested a move date in May so they are busy packing in case it happens.

Bright Lights and Fairy Dust has gained a few more pages since I got back. I'm currently working at a pace that I think I can sustain. If I can keep it up, I should be finished by the end of June. Then I'll be trying to tidy it up and hope to find a potential publisher. But even if I don't get the work published, as Wayne says, 'I'll have the director's cut' which will outlive me and can be handed down to my grand babies as they grow up.

Anyway, that was just a catch up for you.
Love to you both,
Chris

*****

I have continued to work on your cancer diary Darling (*Bright Lights...*) and I finished transcribing June this afternoon. June was particularly special for us because we returned to the Isle of Wight and discovered the Enchanted Manor there. Something touched us as never before and we came home feeling somehow different, although we could not say exactly why.

June was also the month in which we renewed our wedding vows in a moving service at St. John's Church.

In order to write the story of June, I referred to photos, video footage and some of your belongings to help me put down on paper the essence of what we experienced. Writing June, more so than any of the previous months, I felt you were back with me – if only temporarily. The book, after all, is yours and I have often cried on the keyboard as I have recounted our joy and sadness.

I miss you. I don't know what to do to move forward, but I hope that writing *Bright Lights and Fairy Dust* helps us.

*****

I went to a coffee morning in Purley-on-Thames today, arranged through the Duchess of Kent Hospice. I had received a letter in April from the organisers, Genevieve and Lisbeth, explaining how they are 'continually looking to develop their services for the families and carers of those patients who have been in their care'. I ticked the box and a few weeks later another letter arrived explaining that it would be a very informal occasion, with an opportunity to meet with others in similar circumstances. It was only for a couple of hours and I went with an open mind.

Chairs were arranged in several small circles. Attendees were invited to join any circle and to talk to others about their situation and feelings. Two 'facilitators', Holly and Summer, sat in the circle I had chosen. They helped, not by advising, counselling or sympathising, but by keeping things going whenever silence fell.

Although I felt slightly nervous, I wanted very much to speak about you. I wanted to tell people how it had been. I wanted, if I can say this without upsetting you Darling, to 'offload'. And I learned of the others' situations. Pat's husband died from lung cancer; Andy's wife of bowel cancer; Yvette's husband died of motor neurones disease. Rita, who was in our circle initially, was so overcome with emotion that she couldn't speak and felt she had to leave the group. We didn't see her again.

The morning was interesting and informative and I found that it gave me strength, opening up in the company of others.

At the end of the session, we were asked if we would like to join a Bereavement Support Group and meet again later in the year. At that particular moment I wasn't sure if I wanted to.

*****

I returned to Acorn Ridge on what might have been the hottest day since you died. It was still only May, but it was beautiful there. The sky was vivid blue and the hills, to the south and west, were clear and in detail. A cuckoo called in the distance and nearby trees hosted birdsong beautiful enough to be worthy of any garden centre CD.

I took clippers for the first time, because I wanted to tidy the area around your stone.

*****

I can't work out why I am so desperately sad today. What I mean, is I can't determine the specifics of my gloom, although I know you are at the heart of it.

I did a little tidying up at home this morning and came across some things that brought back sad memories. Perhaps those things have peeled back the layer of protection I have built up, exposing my grief to me like an open wound. Maybe it will always be an open wound but one that, for most of the time, will have a dressing on.

I miss you, Darling.

*****

I sent a letter to the organisers of the previous week's Bereavement Coffee Morning:

Dear Genevieve and Lisbeth

I just wanted to write to you to thank you both very much for organising the coffee morning last week. I had meant to write earlier but events this week seem to have overtaken me.

I wasn't sure what to expect, and it was a leap of faith for me to even make the trip, but I had the idea that I might benefit from talking to others who had lost their life-long partners to terminal disease.

As much as I have had (and continue to have) the utmost support from professionals, family and friends, following the death of my Darling Linda last September, I've often felt that very few people actually know the pain of a mate dying; even fewer to one dying from an inoperable disease. Throughout our lives, and especially as we grow older, people dear to us die, and I appreciate that people grieve in different ways according to their relationship, the cause of death and the 'grand order of things'. What was so important about your coffee morning was that you brought together many people whose circumstances were similar. Hearing what others had to say has helped me to appreciate that my thought processes, during Linda's illness, at the moment of her death, and in the eight months since, are all normal. Whilst many others have assured me that they are, speaking and listening to similarly bereaved partners has been a great help.

Thank you once again for your support.

Yours sincerely,
Chris Page

*****

It's getting harder to write *Bright Lights and Fairy Dust*. There is much more text in your drug diary for me to refer to now, but it is a lot tougher on me. Converting all the notes, appointment cards, diary and calendar entries, slips of paper and various scribbles, as well as the contents of my head, into a centralised piece of text that I hope will one day be published, has enabled me to see some things in a different light or, at least, from a different perspective.

As I transcribe the entries, I am forced to recall the not-so-good days of your illness, when pain gnawed away at you every single day, when swelling pushed on your nerve pathways and when muscle wastage began to seriously restrict what you could do. Slowly, gradually, it took your independence away.

I remain in awe of your strength of spirit, Linda. Whatever else was happening, nothing was ever going to take that from you.

*****

I went back to the Day Therapy Unit at the West Berkshire Community Hospital. Today is Wednesday, the day of the Lifestyle Group that you used to attend there.

In the main area, they have had a huge tree painted across the entire far wall. Patients are encouraged to decorate a leaf, which can be stuck to the tree. You never got to see the tree, but I had been invited (or I might have invited myself) to decorate a leaf in your memory. Each one is about six inches long and cut from thick, clear plastic. Some are already on the tree and each one says something about the 'owner'.

Together with others in the Lifestyle Group, I took my place at the table, where a hot melt glue gun oozed adhesive from its muzzle. I took one of the clear plastic leaves and set to work. Because you were such a great communicator, I glued the cover of an old phone on to it. Behind the screen, though, I had placed a photograph I had taken of a message on another phone. It was the title of the book, your story: *Bright Lights and Fairy Dust*. Then, because you so loved your garden, I glued artificial sweet pea flowers around it. Finally, I brought it all together with a tiny watering can and a bow of your favourite colour, lime green.

While at the Unit, I looked in on Roland, who was now in a side room on the adjacent ward. You and I got on well with him and his wife, Josephina. There was usually some banter or laughter among us all at the Unit and they were always up for some of that.

Roland has a brain tumour, as you know.

His leaf had only recently been placed on the tree and had a nautical theme because he had served as a Royal Marine. When I saw him at the Unit two weeks ago, he told me he had been admitted to the ward because he has lost the use of his legs. While there, he picked up MRSA and it was because of this that he was in the side room. He also had a leg ulcer now and both his legs were heavy with fluid. He was semi-recumbent on the bed and I could see that his abdomen was distended, as was the left side of his forehead. The cancer was surely about to take him, but equally the infection might do so. He was being barrier nursed and, as a visitor, I had to don an apron and gloves before going in. He made a point of telling me that I wasn't allowed to shake his hand, but he acknowledged me and thanked me for popping in.

Witnessing his deterioration was very sad and I was close to tears as I thought of you, my Darling. What Roland was going through was exactly what you had wanted to avoid by choosing to be nursed at home. We were proud of the fact that you didn't get an infection, or MRSA, or pressure sores.

I don't think I will see Roland again; they want to move him into a nursing home.

He will die soon.

*****

'Doesn't he look well?'

'You do look well, Chris.'

I don't trust remarks like this and I had another, similar, compliment this morning:

'You look better than when I last saw you.'

Surely, these people can see that I have lost weight and that my face is pinched and drawn. I would rather someone told me that I looked like shit than pretend everything's okay, with the aim of cheering me up. Over the past couple of months, I have lost almost a stone in weight. I think I'm putting a bit on again now.

But I do look like shit.

*****

I have one more day to write up in *Bright Lights and Fairy Dust*. Every day that I get nearer to finishing the work seems to become more and more difficult for me. Tomorrow, I shall be typing out your last day with us. How will I write about your death?

I'm going to need your help.

*****

It has taken me two days to write about one: the day you died.

So often, I could barely see the keyboard through the tears that I cried. And yet, as punishing and upsetting as it has been for me, I continued because it is so important to me that I tell your story. It might take years to get it out there to a wide audience, but that is the next stage. I have no doubt there will be lots of edits and re-drafts, but the sense of achievement that I felt today, when I finally decided that the book was finished, was such that I want to do it. I love you, Dolly.

*****

Another first. There aren't many left now that September is only two months away. Today would have been your birthday, your fifty-eighth to be precise. I took a lavender plant to Acorn Ridge and planted it there for you. This wasn't something I thought I would ever do, because the rules of the site don't allow it, but today I was a maverick. I have to say, the plant looked good.

I trimmed and tidied the grass then went back to the car to get water for the plant and a card I had bought to go with it. The feeling I got in my stomach when I couldn't find the car keys and realised I'd locked them in the boot was awful. I was a long way from anywhere (which was always one of the lovely things about the place) and wondered how I was going to get out of this one. To compound my situation, my mobile phone was also in the boot and I reckoned I would have to walk to Mum and Dad's to enlist their help. On the off chance that I might have dropped the keys when walking across the field, I doubled back towards the lavender. I saw a woman. She was close to your spot. I don't know where she had come from, because I didn't hear anyone arrive, but when I knew beyond doubt that my keys were in the car boot and not in the grass, I walked up to her with the best smile I could manage in the circumstances.

'This will sound like the daftest of questions in a place like this, but you haven't got a mobile phone I could use, have you?'

I explained what I had done.

'As a matter of fact I have. I'm afraid it's a bit basic,' she said, handing it to me.

'It's exactly the same as mine. Thank you. Thank you so much.'

I called Mum and asked for her help. She collected me from Acorn Ridge and took me home. I knocked next door and Pete let me into our house with the spare key he keeps. Then I grabbed the spare car key from the pantry and Mum drove me back to Acorn Ridge. What a silly maverick!

Your birthday really was *memorable*.

*****

I was expecting the drive to Wayne and Sara's to take about two and a half hours. In the end, it took four. By the time I arrived I was frayed. My air-conditioning – temperamental at the best of times – didn't work when I needed it most. Sitting in the car, virtually parked on the motorway in the heat of the middle of the day, with only a bag of wine gums and Radio 4 for company, was far from enjoyable.

When the queue of traffic, which must have stretched for miles, got to the next motorway junction, there was evidence of an earlier accident, the probable cause of the disruption. A stationary articulated lorry, its front smashed in, was in Lane One immediately behind a dark-coloured people carrier (or hatchback – it was hard to tell) with its rear end crumpled severely. It had clearly been more than a touch and so there must have been casualties. It was also, therefore, possible that the accident had initially stretched across several carriageways when it happened.

Someone once told me that whenever an accident held them up, they would always say aloud, 'I'm thankful that's not me'.

It brought home to me again how quickly one's life can change.

*****

Some time ago, I spoke with Wayne and Sara about the Isle of Wight. I thought they might like to stay at The Enchanted Manor with me. I would like to show them some of the places that you and I enjoyed. It's early July and although your babies can only stay for two nights, they will at least be able to share the experience of our favoured holiday destination.

I met them in the car park next to the ferry terminal at Southampton and our journey began. I thought I would feel differently. I was in equal measure pleased that I was returning, but sad that you weren't with us. You too would love to have shared our island with Wayne and Sara.

After driving off the ferry at Cowes, I led the way – the long way – clockwise round the island to the Enchanted Manor. On the way round, we stopped at The Lifeboat in Bembridge, had lunch then walked along the beach, taking in the views. I wanted happy memories to come back, but we all know you can't always get what you want.

I was proud to be showing our island off and hoped that Wayne and Sara were enjoying it, but I also knew I had only a fragile hold on my emotions.

When we reached the Enchanted Manor I was immediately under its spell again. There is something there that draws me in. It is something I feel within me;

that I cannot put across in words. Wayne and Sara will have their own thoughts on the place, but I'm sure that 'comfortable' will be among them.

The owners, Ric and Maggie, were pleased to see us all and delighted with the book on Faerie that I gave them in your memory.

I had a different room from the one you and I shared, but the warmth and feeling of belonging were just the same. It's lovely. It's enchanting.

The next day, we went for a drive and dropped in on Ventnor. I struggled to hold back my tears as we walked along the Esplanade to the Spyglass Inn. Memories, that you and I had made there a year earlier, flooded my head and stung my eyes. I looked back along the beach. It felt like only yesterday.

*****

As I said, your babies could only stay two nights, but my time with them was special. Alone now, I have decided to walk from the Enchanted Manor to Ventnor along the cliffs and the undercliff and return by way of the coast path and the road.

This morning's weather is not very good. I keep coming to the edge of the cliffs. The very edge. There are no railings or barriers and I cannot keep from thinking how easy it would be to slip, or fall. Or jump. Then I think of the likely outcome of such an event and I am horrified. If the victim didn't die, what terrible injuries might they sustain?

Oh, Darling, when I start to think of our time on the island and how uncomfortable you were, how racked with pain, how swollen and immobile, I feel overwhelmed with sadness for what you went through. I was approaching the Botanic Gardens, which you loved, but you were very ill when we went there and my mind now, it seemed, focused only on your suffering. I felt a lump in my throat and a very real sensation that I wanted to throw up. What is causing my body to react in such a way to my mental images?

I stood at the top of the steps that lead down to the sea and cried as the memory of our visit there last year filled my head. You, taking pictures with your mobile phone as you sat helpless in your wheelchair, your legs full of fluid and your body full of cancer. You wanted to go down for a better view and I had to suggest, gently, that it wasn't possible. Even if I had managed to help you down, it would have been impossible to help you back up. It wasn't called Steephill Cove for nothing.

*****

Memories then, they are what it comes down to now. All I have left are my memories, photographs and a few home videos. I feel that I need more; they are not enough. I want so much to come to terms with my situation. I know, as a rational human being, that life has to go on – my life – but mine isn't making sense to me. I pine for you, Darling, such that I often think my heart will break. My sadness, though often masked these days by polite conversation and time spent with family and friends, is always only just below the surface, the mask a thin veil that I'm sure everyone can see through when the conditions are right.

*****

I had to do it: I had to go there. I had covered so many of the places that you and I had been that I felt Yarmouth should be on the list, too. It was difficult for me. I cried. I went to Fort Victoria and walked around the area, calling to mind our visits there. Then, I drove to Norton Grange and sat for a while with more of my memories. Why won't the good ones come? Why are the clearest memories those that bring back the sadness and the heartbreak?

I went into Yarmouth and walked on to the pier. When you were very ill, we had a special Valentine's weekend at a hotel near the Lymington ferry terminal and went over to the island as foot passengers. I say 'foot', but we took your wheelchair and I pushed you all the way to the end of the pier. All I could see today was you in that chair, dressed in your thick, black coat and mohair hat against the cold, February air.

I walked along to The Wheatsheaf to remind myself that on that same day I 'parked' you on double yellow lines, while I went in to see if they could accommodate us for a meal. That was when a customer, who'd seen you outside in the chair, exclaimed, when you walked in after him, *'Sweet Jesus, you're a flipping miracle'*. You put him right, in your usual straight-talking manner, and told him you were *'dying nicely, thank you'*. Now, *that* was a moment to remember.

I am exhausted now, I think by the exertions of my mind's eye. I'm so fatigued that I could fall asleep.

*****

Back at home a poem came into my head and straight away I typed it into the computer, because I didn't want to lose it.

My Darling Linda

I exist; I am alive. I coexist, but I do not thrive.
I have a widowed life. How I love my wife.
I miss her, long to kiss her.
To feel her touch I ache so much. Pining and whining, aching and breaking, these are my prerogative, but they're all negative.
She is gone and I have to get on. I have to endure life without her until death comes to me and we can then be together forever.

*****

Some weeks ago I bought a tin of paint for the downstairs doors. It's satin 'Cream White' and I was sure you would approve. But I never cracked it open; just left it on the kitchen counter. After weeks of looking at it every time I walked into the kitchen and thinking, 'I must do that some time', I put it away in the pantry today.

I just can't summon the enthusiasm.

*****

How did you manage to keep smiling, Darling? I am alive and yet I don't think I smile as much as you did when you were dying. You were amazing.

I love and miss you.

*****

One of your endearing qualities, for me anyway, was your straight talking. I loved the fact that anyone and everyone could be sure of an almost instant answer straight from your heart. If you didn't like something you would say so and if you had an opinion you would give it. People always knew where they stood with you, even if they didn't always like what they heard.

In the later stages of your cancer, when you and I had taken to staying downstairs and we knew things were bad, we often talked of what the future might hold for me. However, all the time I still had you I wasn't very good at trying to see what was beyond the divide. The thought of having to live without you filled me with dread and sorrow. You, though, as much as we were so in love, understood that my life would have to go on. You wanted me to carry on, to move on. And if the situation had been reversed I know would have wanted the same for you.

I recall a brief exchange we had one day:

'You ought to get yourself a dog, Chris,' you suggested to me from your bed. 'It'll be good for you.'

'No, Darling.' I replied, 'I couldn't have another dog. I couldn't bear it. I remember what I was like when Burma died. I couldn't go through that again.'

Without hesitation you came straight back.

'Does that mean you won't get another wife?'

It was a question that has haunted me ever since.

I love you, Linda, and your passing has left me completely shattered.

I didn't answer your question at the time and I'm not sure if I can answer it now.

*****

I had been shopping at our regular supermarket. I hadn't bought much, so I was able to carry it home in bags. As I walked alongside the store towards the main road I saw the woman who used to see us shopping together every week and who always stopped us to ask how we were. Neither of us knew her very well, but she had become a familiar face among the staff and we were always happy to exchange greetings and, sometimes, a little bit of news or gossip. She knew you had died.

'Oh, hello,' she said brightly, upon spotting me. 'How are you?'

'I'm okay, thank you,' I ventured in reply.

'It seems funny, seeing you without a wheelchair.'

'I'd much rather be pushing the wheelchair,' I told her.

'Really? You miss her that much?' Her tone appeared to change to one of surprise.

In my head I forgave her insensitivity, for how could she know my grief, my pain? After all, you and I had only ever been just another couple in a busy supermarket. No one, not even this woman, knew our situation, not properly. We would engage anyone in polite conversation, and you would say that you were 'doing okay' or that you were 'a bit tired', but you never gave too much away. Even when I pushed you round in your wheelchair you still had such a positive attitude. It was always me who was the pessimist, the worrier, the person for whom the glass was always half empty.

'Ahh,' the woman went on. It was the same sort of 'ahh' I might expect to hear from someone peering into a baby's pram; a *that's so sweet* kind of 'ahh'.

The torment continued.

'Still,' she said, 'she's in a better place now.'

I wondered if this woman was expecting me to agree with her. What she had done, in truth, was tumble into a hole – of her own making – and now she was in the process of digging herself out of it. I'm not even sorry to say that I continued to leave her to it.

'At least she's not in pain,' she went on. 'You wouldn't want her to be in pain, would you?'

You had endured pain every day for nine months and every day I wished that I could take it away, or that the drugs would hold it off, but nothing worked for very long.

It was time for me to hold out a hand, help this woman out of her pit.

'No,' I replied. 'No, I wouldn't.'

*****

I got 'a whiff of olden days'. This morning I was in our garden when a sudden and pungent aroma of cigarette smoke cast me back forty-five years or more. I instantly visualised the lounge of my grandparents' home, where a large table stole most of the space from the middle of the room. Around it, on hard, wooden chairs, sat many of the adults in our family. Nan and Grandad, my Dad and some of my Aunties and Uncles were each stuck to a hand of cards and a cigarette. The air in the room was a thick blue haze.

All those years ago, if my sisters and I were to be allowed to stay in the smoke-filled room, we had to be quiet and play our own games. I would occasionally cast a glance at a hand of cards without the faintest idea what any of them meant. I was intrigued by the fancy patterns on the back, tattoo-like in their detail and, on the front, the four different symbols laid out neatly in their numbered patterns. I didn't know what spades and clubs were, but hearts and diamonds were easy enough to grasp. The strange upside down, right-way-up, back-to-front picture cards particularly fascinated me. I used to associate them with cigarettes and alcohol, although I didn't know what alcohol was at the time. I mean, I didn't know that Mackeson – the frothy, fizzy, dark-coloured liquid in the glasses on the table – was alcohol. I knew it was called beer, but I didn't know that beer contained alcohol. If there were ever any sudsy dregs in the bottom of a glass, we might be allowed a sip, so we could be grown up like everyone else. I remember now that it didn't taste very nice.

As I came back to reality, I still didn't know where that smell had come from.

And to this day, I don't know why one of the picture cards is called a 'Jack'.

*****

It's already late July. I don't know where the time has gone, Dolly. I've been organising a Memorial Service for you and working on text and pictures for the order of service. I have often felt that I never really took part in your funeral, that I missed it because my emotions were running so high. I think it will be good to go back to church in your memory. There were some people who were unable to get to your funeral. They might like to come to a Memorial. Others who did come might have similar thoughts to mine. I'd like it to be a celebration of your life. I want it to be happy;

I want to be part of it, just as I am part of you and you are part of me. I don't know, but it may even help me heal.

It's only two months away.

*****

I finished our rose arch and trellis today. It's taken me a few days and I got covered in fence paint, but I think the features are what you wanted in our garden. I shall plant some climbing roses in October. I have read that now is not the time.

*****

I e-mailed Wayne and Sara:

Howdy folks,

The minutes are ticking by. Soon I shall be cooped up in a big metal bird for half a day, heading for Sin City and 42 degrees.

Here, as promised, is the [Memorial] guest list so far. I dropped some invitations into the surgery yesterday, but I think I'm going to leave all the other 'nursey' ones for now and send them all out in one week. Do add to the list if it's obvious that I have left someone out.

You might like to have a look at this little video clip. It came into my head yesterday but I couldn't think who the detective was until this morning. Then I Googled it.

It's Robert Urich as Dan Tanna in the seventies TV show, 'Vega$'.

Hope to speak to you later today.

Love
Popsispackin
xx

America 2

My decision to go to Las Vegas was quite impulsive.

Having already been to America in the spring, I had no plans for a return this year. This outing has come about because our neighbour's daughter is twenty one this year. Trevor, her dad, had been on at me for ages to join the family celebrations in Las Vegas. And I had been saying for ages, 'No, I couldn't justify the expense'.

However, during one of these exchanges over a pint in our local, I eventually blurted out a 'Yes'. Sod the money, I thought. That you died so young might also have got me thinking that I should live for the moment.

Anyway, everything's booked and we leave tomorrow. Jackie's driving the Nissan up to airport parking somewhere near Gatwick, from where we'll be bussed to the terminal and then there'll be a stretched limo waiting for us when we land in Las Vegas.

We're all booked into the MGM Grand. By 'all', I mean there are ten of us in the birthday party. I've already bought a gift for Beth's special birthday and I'll take that with me.

It's kind of them to let me tag along. I've had very little to do except book my flights and the hotel.

*****

Darling, you might not be interested to know this, but I'll tell you anyway. You'll appreciate, though, that it's just the sort of thing that I would pick up on! My seat on the plane was right at the back, where the curve of the tail changes the layout from three seats abreast to just two. I sat next to a young man who was going home to Nevada. He was good company and we chatted a lot.

Now, one of the advantages of my position on the aircraft was that there was a wide floor space directly behind our seats, in which I could pace around whenever I felt cramped. My hosts, on the other hand, I saw resorted to walking laps of the cabin to keep from seizing up. However, they had the edge over me when we came in to land at McCarran. Their position, just about over the wings, was probably the most stable in what I supposed were cross winds. Either that or it was a poor landing. My American friend and I lurched from side to side as the tail of the aeroplane flicked back and forth all the way down to the ground and even as we went along the ground.

It's funny, thinking back, I remember feeling uneasy with all the yawing, but at the same time resigned to a notion of 'what will be, will be'.

The officer checking my travel documents offered me some advice.

'Your first time in Vegas, I guess,' he noted. 'You might want to think about what you're wearing, sir. It's forty degrees outside, and you have a jacket on.'

It's true I was wearing my cream linen jacket, but only so that I had pockets for spectacles, mobile phone, wallet and passport and so on. When we walked out to the limo, I realised immediately what he meant. It was hot, Linda. I mean, really hot. But it was beautiful.

*****

I wondered what was in store for us. We were only staying there for a week and I certainly hadn't gone for the gambling. I'd been told that there was plenty to see and do without sitting down at a crap table or playing a machine.

The MGM Grand lived up to its name. With well over 5,000 rooms, at the time of our visit it was the biggest hotel in the country. The foyer there – like most foyers in Vegas, I was to discover – was the size of a UK dance hall. Near the foyer was a lion habitat, where 'real MGM lions' roamed. We walked through a Plexiglas tunnel on our way through the complex. Often, there would be at least one lion sitting or lying on the top of the tunnel.

Las Vegas was like nothing I have ever experienced and I was intoxicated by everything around me. But there was nothing in my room except a bed, a TV and a place to hang my clothes. No tea or coffee making facilities; no biscuits. The accommodation didn't even include a breakfast, so that meant a visit to Denny's or Starbucks each morning.

On Beth's birthday, the ten of us went for a meal at a restaurant in the concourse beneath the Grand. I presented her with a modestly sized Steiff Bear that I'd bought in Newbury. I think I'd bought it not just for her, but for her children when the time is right, and to pass on down the years.

I found the whole experience of Las Vegas amazing. Every day we walked into and through some of the casinos on the strip, each one with a different theme. To me, it was like a vast fairground for adults, where everything and nothing was real. For instance, I noticed that part of The Paris wall had come away, revealing the 'bones' beneath the 'skin'. It was like a stage set; everything around me was. But the themes interested me and I just wanted to soak up all that I could in this crazy place. Upstairs, in The Venetian, was a water-filled canal where gondoliers sang to their customers as they went along the waterway. Across the street, at Treasure Island, a pirate show was put on in the evening, and one of the boats would actually sink. I sat in on a show at Circus Circus, went to the top of the Eiffel Tower, watched the flamingos (guess where), the fountains at The Bellagio, the base jumpers at The Stratosphere and, of course, the 'real MGM lions'.

Everywhere you go in Las Vegas there is someone trying to sell you a trip to the Grand Canyon and I suppose one can't come all the way out here without going 'up the road' to see it. Some visitors like to do the helicopter ride. We went with a company called Pink Jeep Tours and rode in a ten-seat pink Tour Trekker. We were picked up outside the Grand at six in the morning. After one brief stop at Hoover Dam we crossed from Nevada into Arizona (two more states, Darling!) and arrived at the Grand Canyon before the morning ran out. I'm not sure what I expected to see. It was, like everything else here, a new experience. In only a couple of places, looking down into the canyon, I managed to make out a tiny bit of the Colorado River.

We'd already crossed that back at Hoover Dam, but I would see a lot more of that later in the week.

I still can't get my head around the statistics of this wonder of nature. It's 277 miles long, more than a mile deep and in places up to 18 miles wide. When the early settlers heading west came to the rim, what must they have thought? *That's a mighty big hole, folks. Maybe we should go around it.'* Some detour that would have been!

Although the weather was sunny and warm, the air was different there in the National Park. It wasn't as dry as on the strip. And, because of that, we had bugs; tiny flies that we could only slap at when they landed on us. We never had any in Vegas.

It didn't seem long after we arrived at the Grand Canyon that we were back in the pink Tour Trekker heading back to our hotel. The light was fading as we dropped down from Boulder into Las Vegas. I was tired, but I had enjoyed every moment of the day.

One evening, we all went downtown to Fremont Street. This was another attraction not to be missed and was where the opening credits of *'Vega$'* were filmed all those years ago. Now closed to traffic, it hosts the Fremont Street Experience, where the animated light and sound show along the Space Frame draws the visitors' eyes and ears upwards for a spectacle to behold. Oh, Darling, how we would have enjoyed all this together.

Something that might not have interested you, though, was my intention to visit the National Atomic Testing Museum. During the 1950's, just sixty five miles away in the Nevada Test Site, atmospheric (open air) nuclear bomb testing was carried out. Evidence of this, and underground testing, can be seen in the many craters that now exist out in the desert. I knew I wouldn't get to see these, but I thought it would be interesting to visit the museum.

It was less than two miles from the strip, so I was sure I could walk there easily. It was hot outside, as usual, so I made sure I had a bottle of water with me. I walked alongside Bally's but as soon as it and the strip were behind me I suddenly felt vulnerable. Remember the 'gunman' in New Jersey, Doll? I didn't see anyone else walking along this route. Compared to the hubbub of the strip, I was now on a quiet back road and I was uncomfortable. I turned back. I'll visit the museum next time I come here.

On my last day in town, our group split up and we did our own thing. I'd seen signs for 'Dam Tours' and, once again acting on impulse, decided I wanted to see some more of this marvel of engineering. I bought a ticket in one of the booths on the strip and met my tour bus at the back of The Excalibur.

I had a great time. Built during the Great Depression, between 1931 and 1936, Hoover Dam was sited at Black Canyon on the Colorado River. A city (Boulder) was built to house workers, who worked shifts around the clock. Concrete was poured non-stop for two years, to make the dam 'in one piece' so to speak. And in the turbine hall the Art Deco designs are superb. I was merely one of many 'dam tourists' and they will keep coming to see this amazing place.

Can I just mention, Darling, that there was one hotel and casino in particular that I didn't go in? You know I don't do Egypt. I have no doubt that it would have freaked me out to have put one foot inside the pyramid. Groundbreaking design or not, The Luxor was not for me.

*****

Back home from Las Vegas now, I felt terribly sad again. What is it that brings me down?

I was at the computer today, working on *Bright Lights and Fairy Dust*, and I just kept crying. Through my tears I looked at the screen and asked myself how I managed even to get this far with it.

*****

In my Vegas hotel room, I chatted with you and said how you would have loved it there, but that you and I would not have been able to go. I said it was only because you had died that I could afford the trip. How cruel, how sad, that because I am widowed I was able to take part in an experience that I would love to have shared with you. But then again, perhaps I did just that. I took you with me. I just didn't realise it at the time.

I love you, Linda; wish you weren't gone from here.

*****

I received another letter today about the Bereavement Support Group I'm going to join. Yes, I have decided to try it. They sent me a registration form with details, bullet points and also what I will describe as a questionnaire.

The course (that is what it sounds like to me) will run for eight two-hour sessions and will be at Purley-on-Thames again. These are the bullet points:

- *The aim of the group is to assist bereaved people to address and work through their grief and other issues arising from their bereavement, supporting and being supported by members of the group.*
- *Together, people in the group can share feelings, experiences, insights and understanding and develop ways to cope.*
- *Two trained, experienced Family Support Coordinators will lead the group.*
- *The group will be a closed group – that is the membership of the group remains the same for the duration of the group. The group will have 8-10 members.*
- *The group will run for 8 two hour sessions over an agreed period and then close.*
- *There is no charge for this group.*

I filled in the form not only with my details, but with yours too. I was asked for the date you died; your relationship to me; your age; the cause of your death. These were very direct questions, which I reasoned that they had to be, but as I filled in the boxes I felt a jolt at each response.

Overleaf were three large empty text boxes on one A4 sheet and I had to complete each one in response to the question above it. I hope what I wrote doesn't upset you, Darling. Here we go:

What do you feel are your present needs regarding your bereavement?

I don't think that I am 'stuck' in grief (when I consider how I was six months ago, I am sure I am stronger now) but I often feel that I'm in a fog, searching for something. Unfortunately for me, I don't know what that something is. Perhaps, when I find it, only then will I know what it is that will help me into the continuing stages of my bereavement.

What do you hope to get from a Bereavement Support Group?

Perhaps, by talking with other bereaved people I will get an understanding of what it is I'm searching for in the fog. Do they feel the same? What has helped them? Maybe all I can hope for is some reassurance that I'm not going crazy. Beyond that, I do not know.

Please indicate anything else you would like us to know about yourself.

I was a member of the emergency services for eleven years: I was a policeman for five and a paramedic for six. That was a long time ago. I mention this because I want you to know that I have seen death many, many times. I have been first on scene at a murder and I have had people die in front of me. I have coped with the physical and physiological aspects of death without the need for counselling. NOW, though, things are different.

I posted everything off today. The first session is at the end of September.

*****

I could never 'bank' sleep; could never catch up on late nights.

The more sleep I try to get, the more depressed I seem to get.

Jet lag. Wayne had told me that it would be bad, coming back from the western USA. I hadn't thought so initially. I could go to bed at 10.30 p.m. and would go straight to sleep. However, I had a hard job getting out of bed at 6.30 in the morning. In Las Vegas, that's 11.30 at night. Sort of bed time.

Today, I have been home for exactly one week. Am I back to normal? It doesn't feel like it.

*****

I expect that when visiting the grave of a dear relative, most people take flowers or a plant. I took grass.

I've taken grass seed before, but today I took grass, a turf I bought at the garden centre. I wanted to narrow your grave and I think it has worked. Suddenly, you are slimmer. When your grave was dug, it was according to the funeral directors' specification that you had a three-foot-wide coffin. It was a ridiculously big hole. Now, just by splitting this turf into nine-inch strips and laying one either side of the hump, I think your grave is much better proportioned.

*****

Yet again, I travelled a very long way for some memories. It was just after five o'clock in the afternoon when I sat on the rocks at Spekes Mill Mouth, on the north Devon coast. The tide was in, or coming in. I looked down into the bay and watched two beach anglers launch their bait earnestly into the Atlantic froth. A kestrel hovered overhead – no doubt looking for food – and I was reminded of the times we came here with our dog, Burma, when the tide was out of course, when we would go out on to the sand bars and play with him. It wouldn't have been possible in today's conditions. It was windy and the sea was white with foam and a long way in. The sky, though, was blue and the sun shone, glinting from time to time off the bejewelled breakers as they crashed down.

The forecast for the next day was awful but I was pleased, really pleased, to have made my pilgrimage and to call to mind wonderful times with you.

Something we didn't do was walk from here to the Hartland Quay Hotel, so I've decided to do that. It is about a mile away. Our car is parked just back from Speke's Mill, somewhere near Kernstone, on a soft, muddy bank near a sign that reads, 'Unsuitable For Motors'. I can see the rough track beyond the sign.

I will have something to eat at the hotel and then wend my way back to the car.

The Hartland Quay Hotel was exactly the same as I remember it; as you would have remembered it. And why wouldn't it be? However, it was another of those moments that filled my head with a range of emotions when I got there and walked in. There was sadness, because you weren't with me; a feeling of 'achievement', because I had actually done it; perhaps there was even 'closure', because going there enabled me to sit, to reminisce, assure myself that I *could* go on.

The alternative, I suppose, is never to return to the places we shared, but I wonder how I might be affected by avoiding everything and everywhere that we enjoyed as a couple.

I do not want my memory of you to fade but at the same time, I think in order for me to take little steps forward, perhaps I have to box up stuff like this. It hurts. It hurts very much.

As I sat outside the hotel and waited for my chicken and vegetable curry to arrive, I watched families and couples doing exactly what we used to do. Exactly what we would be doing now: enjoying the remains of a beautiful day, contemplating the beauty and power of nature and the achievements of humankind. Our Hartland, that little time capsule we stumbled across all those years ago, appeared unchanged and, right then, I knew I could come back again.

After my curry, I climbed up to the village of Stoke, walked past St. Nectan's church and called at the B&B. I announced my arrival because I had told the landlady in an e-mail that I would be with her around 6.30 p.m. and I didn't want to mess her around.

As I described earlier, the car was parked near a sign 'Unsuitable For Motors'. It took me a further 45 minutes to walk back to the car along the winding, stony lane and I can confirm that the sign at the other end is most appropriate. I drove back along more sensible roads to my accommodation and settled in for the night.

At breakfast the next morning Fiona, the landlady, engaged me in conversation and asked what I did for a living. I explained my situation and that I hadn't worked for almost two years. But, I said, I was thinking of working for myself; just didn't know yet what that would be.

She made some fresh tea, sat down at the table with a pen and some paper and started to brain storm, listing a whole lot of jobs that she thought I could look into, based on what I'd told her about my past.

Fiona wrote, 'Think small jobs, added together'; 'locksmith (feed on from your carpentry jobs)'; 'pest control'; 'installing loft insulation for the elderly'.

'You could call yourself *The Handy Husband*,' she said.

I wasn't sure about the use of the word husband but replied that she had certainly given me plenty to think about.

*****

They said the weather would be awful; they were right. Rain. Lots of it. And gales to come, too. Not the weather to go walking the coastal path, or to go walking anywhere really so, instead, on the way home from my break, I went to Clovelly for another trip down memory lane. And what an appropriate use of the word *down* that is.

I paid my money, went out through the visitor centre and began the steep descent. The weather ran off my Berghaus jacket and on to my trousers. These – my jeans – not being waterproof, pulled the rain through to my skin, from where it ran down into my shoes and socks. As wet as I was though, I was determined to visit this place and draw on memories of our time there together, years ago. I walked to the end of the harbour wall and looked back at the lifeboat station and the village. I was fascinated by the way the buildings clung to the geography and by how Clovelly must have been built. You and I were here together more than ten years ago. It looks the same, but I know it can't be.

Because you're not here.

My bottom half (including my bottom) was soaked to the skin, but I decided not to take the Land Rover back to the top. I walked instead, hauling my sodden body back up the cobbles and into the visitor centre. I went to the car and pulled some items from my luggage, then went to the gents and changed out of my soaked clothing. I had a long drive ahead.

I think I feel stronger and I think this pilgrimage has been easier to bear. Apart from a brief moment when I thought tears would flow whilst at Spekes Mill Mouth yesterday, I have been more able to deal with my thoughts and emotions.

It doesn't mean I don't miss you. I still ache.

*****

Your Memorial Service is exactly three weeks away. I have put out invitations over the course of several weeks to more than 360 guests (although I do know that many people can't come) and I wonder how many extra chairs we will need in the church.

The invitations I designed have Josephine Wall artwork on, a nod to The Enchanted Manor, and I have echoed this on the cover of the service booklet that I have been producing.

I haven't met the new vicar, whom I understand started in August, but Father Trevor is coming to the house on Saturday evening to run through the service. Trevor, as he prefers to be called, has covered St. John's since Father Bernard retired and he is especially happy to conduct your service because he took your funeral. I spoke to him on Wednesday and, to his relief, I said we wouldn't, after all, be singing the hymn, 'I'll Be A Sunbeam'. The reason I have pulled it is that I am worried that no one will know it. I have replaced it with, 'Give Me Joy In My Heart'.

Yesterday, Wayne and I recorded a song at his studio in Brockley that we hope to play at the end of the Memorial Service. It was one of your favourite songs and I hope you approve of our rendering of Bob Marley's '*Three Little Birds*' and that you know your boys have put it together with all our love. I hope it meets with Trevor's approval, too, along with the other songs and hymns.

*****

It's a beautiful evening. The sky is pale blue and decorated with high and wispy cirrus clouds and the washed out remains of aeroplane vapour trails. The sun is low, the shadow of your grave is long and that of your five-foot hawthorn tree stretches nearly thirty feet across the recently mown grass. High above me – directly above me in fact – on this perfectly dry and warm, late summer evening, is a small rainbow, the presence of which I simply cannot explain. It is long enough that I can see the curve in it, and each end is turned upwards, like a smile. It is not my imagination. Alas, I do not have a camera with me this evening and, anyway, your rainbow's hues are so subtle that a photograph may not capture them. But I did.[3]

I love you, Darling, and I miss you very much.

*****

I sent an e-mail to Wayne, preparing him for the contents of the booklet I've been producing for your service. It's important to me that there are no surprises that might upset him, but I realise the content might do so anyway. So that he can brace himself, I've put the subject heading in as *'Do not open the attachment in haste'*

Dear Wayne,

I had Trevor with me on Saturday and we're close to buttoning down the service.
He still has to send me a final blessing text that I will include just before 'Three Little Birds'.

I took on board comments that you and Sara made about including the song words and I've also adapted what I already had, following Saturday's meeting.
I told Trevor I would include an additional sheet to accommodate the changes.

Today I have been working on the booklet again. We always knew how beautiful Mum was - well, now she's a real, genuine Centrefold.

---

[3] This phenomenon is called the **circumzenithal arc** and comes about when sunlight is refracted through ice crystals in high clouds, rather than through raindrops. Because it forms in this way, it is not a *rain* bow, but belongs to the family of *halos*.

Be prepared to weep a little (or a lot) when you open the attached PDF but, again, I didn't want to spring any surprises on you on the day.

Let me know what you think, Son.

Love
Poppadom
x

One week later, I sent another e-mail to Wayne and Sara:

Howdy!

My word, this was tougher than I thought.
The content was always there, but I couldn't seem to bat it into shape.
I think this works now, though.

Love to you both,
Poporation
xx

I had sent him the words of my reading. There is now just one week to go and I want to make sure everything's as good as it can be.

*****

It's colder today; cooler anyway. I'm here with you again at Acorn Ridge and as you do your best to warm me through breaks in the cloud, I sit and ponder the reality that in just ten days you will have been parted from me for a year – a whole year.

I wish I could have made your resting place tidier than it is. Over the past months, I have slimmed you down, sown new grass seed, laid turf, planted two lavenders and scattered the area with cowslip seeds from your garden. I have set crocus and snowdrop bulbs in readiness for the spring, cleared the larger stones from the ground as they have been exposed by wildlife and weather and I have kept your stone tablet clear. I still think everything should look better – smoother – but perhaps only time will determine the outcome.

*****

I have never spent longer in a menswear shop than I did today. I must have been in the outfitters in Basingstoke for over an hour, during which I went through at least ten suits or jackets in various styles.

I didn't think I was giving the man a particularly hard time but, after about six combos, he seemed to give up on me and passed me on to another assistant. The second man was more forgiving of my indecision and in a 'softly, softly, catchy monkey' approach, he eventually made a sale. I swapped my cash for a charcoal Daniel Hechter two-piece suit with a 38 inch chest and a 32 inch waist. I still haven't put much weight on, Darling, even after almost a year.

*****

I looked up from tending your plot, my ears picking up on the approaching sounds of animals straining at the leash. I saw a woman with dogs.

'I usually let them off up here,' she said, when she realised they had my attention.

Two pugs, one beige, one black, were huffing and coughing as they pulled hard against her in their chest harnesses.

'Why don't you?' I enquired. 'Or are they vicious?'

'No, it's just that I don't like them to run around when there are people here.'

'Oh, go on,' I said, thinking they were unlikely to bother me.

Even after she'd let them off they continued making their choking noises and she (and they) walked on down to one of the other plots. I went back to my trimming and tidying.

I could hear the dogs approaching me again and thought that they might, after all, have come to investigate the man with the trowel in his hand but, when I looked up, they were in harness again and the lady was heading out with them.

'I wish I knew what was attacking my plants,' she said.

'Rabbits.'

'Oh, is that what it is? I did wonder.'

'Have you got someone here?' I asked, hoping that my question wasn't too impertinent.

'My husband. Seven weeks and six days,' she replied, undisturbed by my inquisition and, actually, apparently happy to let someone else know. 'Is this your wife?'

'Yes. It's coming up to the first anniversary. We're having a Memorial Service on Friday. I just wanted to make sure everything was tidy.'

'I've been admiring this.'

'It's probably overkill,' I said, shyly, and a little embarrassed. Your plot was indeed very neat.

I tried to justify my work. 'I've been mucking about for months. I know there will be people coming here over the next few days.'

I went back to my questioning. 'How did your husband die?'

'Just dropped down dead – in front of the children.'

'Was he ill?' I asked.

'No,' she replied. 'Although he'd had a heart attack once before. He'd had a stent put in, because he'd had a cyst on the artery. No, we were out cycling with the kids and he had a massive heart attack. It was instantly fatal.'

'It's probably the case that the stent was the strongest part of his heart, that something else went wrong.'

She appeared to agree.

'And I've got a brain tumour,' she told me. 'I've been in remission for six years. I thought I'd be the one to go. We got a double plot here, although I've got no intention of joining him just yet. I'm just thinking ahead.'

'What did they do for you – the cancer?'

'Oh, I had treatment in London. At Charing Cross. The consultant there was very straight-talking. A brilliant Oncologist, but I wouldn't want to be his friend. I overheard him once, on the phone to someone. I heard him say, *'I am a nice man, but you've got cancer and you're going to die'*. As I say, straight-talking, but that's exactly what I wanted.'

I was surprised at the volume of information that had just been passed across to me and, I think, I didn't know what to say next.

She foreshortened the pause.

'I'm Nanette,' she said.

I took off my gardening gloves and gave her a gentle handshake.

'And I'm Chris. It's nice to meet you, Nanette.'

*****

With your Memorial Service now just hours away, I sent an e-mail to Father Trevor. I asked if he would make some announcements in church on my behalf, to explain what was going on after the service.

If the weather allowed, I wanted to offer people an opportunity to visit Acorn Ridge. Some guests will have never been there and some who will have travelled a great distance may wish to visit again but won't know how to get there. I was happy to lead a convoy if anyone did want to visit.

There will be refreshments, a finger buffet and a party afterwards at our local. I was thinking that it won't matter if I'm still at Acorn Ridge, people can start without me.

I explained that the pub is going to hold a raffle to raise funds for the Berkshire Cancer Centre, although I don't know what the raffle prizes are. I wanted guests to know that the BCC was pivotal in your ongoing care and treatment during your illness.

And finally, I had asked Father Trevor to announce that the *Boogie Nights* disco team are going to be playing music from the 60s and 70s later in the evening. The choice of disco feels so appropriate for what is, after all, a celebration of you, my love. You were very clued up on the 60s and 70s and knew far more than I did about the music from that era. You could recite whole songs that I hadn't even heard of!

*****

Well, my Darling Linda, I have spent many months planning your Memorial Service and I think during this time I must have worried about every aspect of it: the music, the readings, the numbers of guests and service booklets, the 'reception' (or party), the disco. In the end, though, my fretting was needless because it went off very well indeed. I felt comfortable and confident in my new suit, and you filled the church – again. I would not be surprised to learn that two hundred people attended.

Wayne had done a fantastic job on *all* of the music (not just the track that he and I recorded). Our readings were absolutely right for the occasion and came from our hearts.

This was mine:

> *Linda was wild, passionate and spirited; but she possessed innate warmth and radiance, and had a permanent glow about her that brought light to the darkest of places.*
> *Whether you knew her well, or had only just met her – and although it was often the case that you'd hear her before you saw her – you couldn't escape 'the Linda effect'. She had such a presence.*
> *She lit up my life. Just a glance from her beautiful brown eyes would hold me in thrall. And I know she had a similar effect on most people.*
> *Linda loved life; she was as large as life; and she was **my** life.*
> *I love you, Dolly.*
> *When she knew that she was dying she had wanted to record, on tape, her own eulogy, to be*

played back in Church at her funeral. That was Linda and, as bizarre as the idea sounds now, I wasn't surprised when she told me what she wanted to do. I was even prepared to help her achieve it and I have no doubt that she would have had lots to say to make people smile.

We were dissuaded from making that recording, and perhaps ultimately everyone should be thankful, but Linda remained disappointed that she couldn't tell you in her own words and in her own voice.

Even as a child Linda wanted to take care of others, and when her Dad, who was a soldier, would get in from work, she'd often bandage his head, and his arms, and his legs, as they pretended between them that he'd returned home with war wounds. He was her first patient and she went on to devote her life to nursing. When Linda looked after her 'real' patients it was with pride and a deeply caring attitude.

Throughout her life her enthusiasm – for everything she did – was infectious. She encouraged others; drew the best out of them; got them to believe in themselves. Everyone here has in some way been moved by the way Linda conducted her life and her work.

Despite mankind's continuing failings it is a beautiful world. And although we miss Linda, for all those who had the good fortune to meet her on their own journeys through life, she made a beautiful world a better place.

But she was wanted for a sunbeam. That's what she often told me; and perhaps, after all, that's why she glowed.

And so it is that her light shines on. And, whenever we need it, it will be there for us on the darkest of our days ahead.

When I eventually found the words and music, I wanted to include 'I'll Be A Sunbeam' as one of the hymns in today's service, but I worried that you might not know it, so we're just going to play it to you instead.

If you do know it though, or if you feel like having a go at singing along, the words are in the book.

Thank you.

There were enough service booklets after all, perhaps because we gave out a black and white one with a colour one to couples. As it turned out, there were colour booklets left over. Oh, well, better that than to have run out.

Your service flowed well from beginning to end. However, after the last piece of music had been played – the song Wayne and I had recorded – nobody moved. Such a service seemed to leave everyone wondering what to do next. There was no coffin to follow out of the church. After slightly too long, I stood up, turned to the congregation and called out loudly, 'That's all folks!' Laughter broke out and spontaneous applause filled the church with appreciation not just of the service but also of you. We had come to celebrate you and your Memorial Service had done exactly that.

After the service many went to Acorn Ridge. A friend said there, 'I don't believe in life after death.

You're born; you live; you die'. That might be true (no one knows) but I need my faith. It keeps me going.

Also, some people are clearly awkward when the word *died* or *death* is mentioned. These days, one year on, perhaps I feel less awkward than they do.

You would have enjoyed the party afterwards. The pub was packed and *Boogie Nights* did a great job.

*****

It's Sunday. I got back from Mass just after nine this morning and decided to call Australia. Mum and Auntie Jean have gone out to visit Uncle Doug and our family in Queensland. Uncle Doug is not well.

To my surprise and delight it was Mum who picked up at the other end. Just as I was thinking about them all on the other side of the world, so they were doing the same about the family back here.

'I hope everything's okay', she said. 'We lit a candle and we're all thinking of you.'

*****

It is very still here, at your graveside. The weather, so cold only days ago, is warmer now, cloud cover trapping the air beneath it. The hills in the distance are cloaked in low cloud. On the highest ground, I can see rain falling as tears, shed for you and for us especially on this, the anniversary of your death.

Oh, Darling, I wish I could think of an alternative word, one that feels less celebratory, but nothing comes to mind. I am therefore left to suppose that today's date will always be the 'anniversary'.

As I tend your plot, adding fresh grass seed and clearing handfuls of small stones from the soil I have disturbed, I whisper, 'I love you, Darling,' and 'I miss you so much,' and 'Please give me the strength to carry on, or else come for me.'

Today is painful for me to bear, but I can appreciate now that last Friday, in the cold and damp weather, with a cruel wind attacking us at Acorn Ridge, I took my biggest step in coming to terms with my situation. That was the day of your Memorial Service and I only realise now that it has helped me immensely.

I returned to your resting place at 6.15 p.m. Trish had sent me a text earlier in the day to say that she had a spare air lantern, was going to Acorn Ridge at six and would I like to join her. Although I was a little late, she had waited patiently and we lit the lanterns together. I was nervous as I watched my paper balloon slowly puff out, the lighted fuel packet at its base warming the air inside it. When I let it go, it rose into the sky carrying my wishes and my love to you. My lantern, however, didn't go far and I watched with a degree of worry as it sank to the ground just the other side of the River Enborne, the boundary of Acorn Ridge. Clutching my head with both hands, I was concerned that the fuel packet hadn't gone out and that it would set someone's garden on fire, or the field it was heading for. Trish laughed and tried to convince me that it would be fine. Her lantern made much better progress and we watched it fade well into the distance before it, too, lost lift and fell to earth. It certainly was a 'fun' way to mark today.

*****

I drove to Purley-on-Thames this morning, for my first Bereavement Support group meeting. I can hardly believe it's been four months since I went to the coffee morning there.

There were ten in the group and Genevieve and Lisbeth were the two facilitators who were leading the course. It was good to meet them properly. We sat in what was nearly a full circle, each of us with a hot drink and a biscuit. After the facilitators had settled us in, they asked us to introduce ourselves and explain a little about our bereavement. For me, two things were instantly clear: I could talk openly about you without having to leave anything out (the more upsetting details, I mean) and I realised I wasn't alone in feeling the way I do. I was also surprised at how many people were cared for at home and, although we never attended the hospice at Duchess of Kent House, at what went on in the background there whilst our spouses were fighting terminal illness.

One of the widows spoke to me in the car park after our meeting. Although we didn't know one another, we exchanged condolences and I felt an obvious connection with her simply through our bereavement to cancer.

'They're doing their best but they don't understand,' she said, referring to the facilitators, 'it's about the cuddles, too.'

I know what she means. Today, in our circle, we had poured out our feelings, our grief, but no one had mentioned the absence of physical contact.

On the way home I noticed leaf fall for the first time. It's obviously been going on for a little while, judging by the amount of fallen leaves but, speaking personally, I only noticed today.

The horse chestnuts, which have already been dropping their spiked seed pods in earnest, don't look well. Their leaves are mottled and blackened, their fall to the ground serving only to accentuate their poor looks. Limes are curling at the edges and, unless my eyes deceive me, are beginning to turn colour. The trees on either side of the road alerted me to this annual event. The slightest breeze, or the passing bow wave from approaching traffic, seemed to convince the leaves that it was time to loosen their temporary grip on their host. I have an idea the trees might be maples, but I'm not sure.

It will not be long before the beautiful palette of autumn colour dapples our skylines. Soon enough we shall be left to view only bare branches and a bigger sky as we plod through the forthcoming winter waiting, like the trees, for longer and warmer days.

Then we will all bloom again, in hopes to prosper beneath warm sunshine and the promise of a better year.

*****

With friends, I went to the pub, the same pub that had hosted the refreshments following your Memorial Service exactly one week earlier. There was live entertainment and the place was packed with people, mostly younger than the company I was in now. On every table was a large plate, loaded with something to eat.

We bought our drinks and sat down at one of the tables.

'Nice food,' I said to a person I recognised. 'What's the occasion?'

'Someone's fiftieth.'

'Oh, a proper party then? Who's fifty?'

'That lady there.'

As I looked across the room, I was unsure as to whom I was meant to be looking. I didn't know if I was looking at the right woman.

'She doesn't look fifty.' I paused to finish my egg sandwich. 'This food is great,' I said. 'It's nice to enjoy it, because I didn't get to see the food last week.'

'No, you didn't have any, did you?'

'Never got the chance. I was busy.'

'It's been a year, Chris. Do you feel better now?'

'Gosh, I wouldn't say better. I feel different.'

'Different?'

I wasn't sure I could improve on my answer, so I reworded it and tried again.

'I feel different than I did this time last year. But not better.'

'But you're moving on.'

'Perhaps I am. I have no choice. I have to try to move forward.'

'You might meet someone else.'

At this point, I wanted to switch off the conversation. It wasn't one I wanted to have.

'I don't want someone else.'

'Ah, but you never know. You're a good looking bloke.'

Oh, dear.

I know that people mean well, but some of them just don't know what to say, or how to say it, and they're the ones who would do better to say nothing. I can honestly say I haven't heard a single phrase in over a year that has inspired me. They've all been clichés: 'Time is a great healer.' 'You have to let your grief come out.' 'The first year is the worst.' 'It gets easier.' These are all meant to provide encouragement, but they only underline my situation. I am bereft. You were my life. You were my whole world – are my whole world – I can't just switch that off and re-route my thoughts.

'My old car broke down so I went and got another one. It gets me from A to B. It's not as good as the other one, but it'll do.'

No. I can't do it.

*****

8.20 a.m.

I put the washing machine on, having loaded it with the usual batch of light clothes: shirts, hankies, tees. I set the programme for *Daily Load* and pressed start. I thought – just thought – I heard it make a struggling noise as it came on, but then it got going and I walked away.

I walked back to the machine less than five minutes later and I had a definite feeling that it didn't sound right.

'It doesn't usually make this noise,' I muttered, aloud.

I wondered if the bearings were on the way out, were worn out, or if the drive belt was about to break.

Anyway, I couldn't do anything about it, so I walked away again. Nevertheless, I thought I would jot down my concerns in case it does conk out on me. Then I can mutter to myself, 'I told you so.'

*****

In my waking moments it occurred to me that I didn't have the pain. The pain in my back has been more of a dull ache, but I've had it for weeks now, in particular on my right side. It has gnawed away at me all day, every day. Although I think it's probably just muscular, the thought that it is something more sinister keeps coming into my head. Even so, I don't want to go to the doctor.

Unfortunately, the pain returned shortly after I had showered and got dressed.

Here I go again.

*****

Just as life goes on, so death goes on too. Here I am again, tending your plot, where the grass seed I put down last week has started to sprout. The noise of a small digger, something like a Kubota, chugs away on the last line of the graves, but it isn't digging a grave, it is filling one in. Someone else recently buried here; someone else who has left this earthly plane and their loved ones. By the end of today, there will be a mound of soil on top of the coffin, rather than beside it. In a few months, it will sink a bit, just as yours did. The cycle of life and death is as perennial as the grass I sowed last week. Perhaps it is coming to terms with this fact that has helped me on my own journey through grief. It doesn't mean I miss you any less Linda. Quite the opposite: I miss you every single day and I pine for what we can never have back and for what you and I didn't quite achieve, like retirement, grandparenting, moving to the island. I am desperately sad that you had to leave us all so early in life.

Then, as I look around and witness the growing number of new plots, I see that we were merely statistics in everyday life; just another couple who faced a final farewell far too soon.

By the way, the sun is shining and it is beautiful here today.

Just for now, I bid you 'Goodbye, Darling', but I will be here again soon enough.

*****

When the sky is bright and blue and clear and the sun beats down on us here below, I have started to call such a day a Wagamama day. It gives me comfort to think of the day in terms of one in which you have had a hand.

I need comfort.

The day you were born – always described by you as being a heat wave – was almost certainly one. The day you died was also a Wagamama day. The sun shone into our garden and through the sliding patio doors at the foot of your bed. We tried to let the outside into the house.

You, my Darling, were the light of my life. In the dark days since your passing, I have welcomed Wagamama days. I feel you close to me.

*****

Do you remember, Dolly, how you and I used to talk about who would die first? And we didn't just have one conversation, because it was a subject that came up often and certainly long before your diagnosis. Perhaps it was because of what happened in your family. I am thinking, of course, about your Mum and Dad and

Brenda and David. Perhaps, when we had these chats, you were already thinking that something in the family might predispose you to an early death. Thinking about it some more, we sometimes mulled over the almost unbelievable list of surgery you had already endured. Your abdominal scars virtually mapped out the removal of most things. As well as the hysterectomy to save your life, your appendix, gall bladder and ovaries had also been taken away. And I was with you when you went in as a day case to have cysts removed. Then there was the Morton's neuroma and stripping out your varicose veins. For years, you put up with HRT implants, the pellets pushed in using a trocar the size of a chopstick. You had a terrible time, but you never complained.

So why did I think I would die first? Because I always had pain. Somewhere. Still do. I used to tell you that I have worn out my body with everything I've done in my life. I have an ongoing back problem, which, when it is bad, ages me fifteen years. Each time I get a cold, it seems to be worse than any that I've had before and leaves me with a terrible chest.

Perhaps, if I analyse our conversations deeply, it was the case that I *hoped* I would die first, because I couldn't bear to be here without you. In that regard, nothing has changed.

Since you died, I honestly think that my health has declined further. In my mind, every little problem I have is going to lead to cancer and death. My weight loss and weight gain, my poor motility and my irregularity, lumps in my abdomen, frequent feelings of bloating, palpitations, headaches and the occasional inability to think at all, let alone think straight, make me wonder if something is brewing. I don't mind, as long as I am free of pain. On the plus side, at least I have finished *Bright Lights and Fairy Dust*. It was very important to me that I got that all down before I leave here to be with you.

*****

As I walked back from the supermarket, having first bought a train ticket to London for the next day, a strange thought came to me, an outrageous thought, really. I haven't really had a day off since you were diagnosed, the same day I was made redundant. Sure, I didn't go to work *as such*, but I think I have spent every day doing something.

Perhaps I'm looking at it wrongly, but I don't recall a day since then when I have relaxed and done *nothing*. I looked after you, of course, and I wouldn't have a changed a thing there. But since your death I've worked on the book, the service, planned for trips both at home and away.

I suspect it's actually the case that because I don't have a Monday to Friday job anymore (or any job, come to that) all the days melt together. Even the hours of the day come 'en bloc'. The result? Morning drifts into the afternoon and then the evening, all without institutional breaks like lunch at one or high tea at five. Monday is the same as Friday is the same as Saturday and Sunday. There's no start to the week and no end. When I lump all that together and consider the year that has passed since you died, it's just been one long block of time punctuated by events rather than points on the clock.

It's now 2.30 p.m. and I've just had lunch.

See what I mean?

*****

I was between Thatcham and Theale, on the 8.57 bound for Paddington, off to see Wayne and Sara for the day, when I suddenly remembered that today is our wedding anniversary. At least, it would have been. It would have been our twenty-fifth and, for that reason, as anniversaries go, this one is particularly sad. We had so many plans. We were going to renew our wedding vows (we brought that forward) and you were going to try to scale down your hours, or at least get some quality back to your life, because the long hours and the physical exertion were taking you down.

Thinking back a couple of years, to the time roughly when you found things were much more difficult and required energy you didn't feel you had, I cannot help but consider the possibility that you had the cancer even then but we didn't know it.

Cancer takes time to develop into a matter that takes the patient to a doctor. How long I do not know, but you probably had it even when you were nursing Brenda and David through theirs.

I'm feeling a bit down, Darling. The fact that today would have been our wedding anniversary will have a lot to do with it, but it might also be because I am worried about my weight. Don't laugh, please. I lost almost a stone during your illness then seemed to level out at around 11st.11lb. Now, I am creeping back up again, but all the weight seems to be going on my belly. I often think I can feel a lump there and that I have something growing inside me. I don't want to go to the doctor though. If it turns out to be *that something* then I would rather nature take its course than me go into hospital. I don't want to endure tests; invasive procedures; contrasts; CT; x-ray; biopsy; all that stuff you went through. No thank you. Please, if you can, just make sure I'm free of pain. That's all I ask.

Someone said that's a bloke thing, thinking every little thing is cancer.

Wayne and I went to Rotherhithe, to the Brunel Museum. It's not a big place, located in the old engine house, but big enough to show off the exhibits and accommodate visitors. We had the special privilege of being allowed down into the shaft from where the original Thames Tunnel was started. The entrance was tricky, through a very small opening in the top. Balfour Beatty had left their scaffold staircase on the inside and we went down to the new concrete floor they had only recently installed. We were told that before it was put in, the shaft went all the way down to the underground railway, which we could hear and feel beneath our feet. Both of us felt that you might have worked some of your magic that day, to get us inside the shaft. After all, at the time it was only open on special occasions. Today we were allowed to tag on to an organised tour for about ten people who were on a team-building day out from their work. And through what might have been a health and safety issue – the aforementioned 'hole' – we were visitors to a space that had not been open to the public for 145 years.

Thank you, Darling.

*****

I couldn't let go of much a year ago, but in the past couple of months I have been able to give away some of your clothes that, I could say, defined you. Headbands, cardigans, blouses; even a coat and a salmon-pink fleece have all been 'recycled' within the family. For me, that was better than putting them into a charity shop.

There are some things, though, that I cannot let go of. Not yet. Maybe never. They continue to give me some comfort.

*****

It's already October Dolly and this evening I played at a dance in a big barn. We call it the Black Barn but I think 'Rushall's Barn' is the correct name. I'm sure you've been here with me, at least once. It's tucked away in the Berkshire countryside and surrounded by very little except fields, trees and hedgerows.

It never ceases to amaze me that people turn up at our barn dances in jeans and checked shirts. Tonight there were several cowboy hats and, incredibly, someone even wearing black suede chaps. These people hadn't come to a barn dance, they'd come to a hoedown. Oh, well, perhaps it's all the same thing.

It was cold in the barn, despite having what might have been a hundred people there to warm it with their breath and activity. It was so cold that many of the guests even danced in their coats. Indeed, when we started playing I kept my coat on for a while until I felt ridiculous and took it off. Then I got cold and remained cold for the entire evening. I wasn't simply tapping my foot, or feet, to the music, I was striking the ground hard with my feet, alternating them like a football substitute might do to warm up before going on the pitch. I was shivering, my feet and hands like ice, my nose as cold as a dog's.

When we broke for refreshments, it was, thankfully, a hot meal that was presented, and we warmed ourselves from the inside with the chilli and rice that was served. It was extremely tasty, and well timed.

At the end of the evening, when we packed up and started to take our equipment out to the cars, I felt that the barn was hardly warmer than the fields outside. I looked up at the night sky, which returned sight of a myriad stars because of the absence of neighbours and light pollution. It was indeed beautiful.

'We might have the first frost of the autumn,' I said, as we all loaded up our vehicles.

When we left the venue, the temperature gauge in the car indicated that it was 7 degrees outside. When I got back home to Newbury, it had dropped to 3 degrees.

The next morning everything outside was coated in a thick layer of ice.

*****

I was travelling by train to Brockley, just as I have many times before. Usually, whenever I've walked on to the platform, I have done so without being challenged. Sometimes, on the train, the Train Manager has asked for my ticket, but not always. Even after he has blurted out the itinerary in a joined up mumble of irritating and patchy dialect, he hasn't always bothered to patrol the carriages.

This morning, as I crossed the threshold from the ticket office to the platform, three uniformed officials were waiting. Dressed in long, dark coats, they were bunched together like nightclub doormen. One of them lunged at me with a soulless face and an outstretched hand.

'Ticket please.'

Whilst it could be argued that the 'please' made his request a polite one, I couldn't help wondering where such employees receive their training. I was sure there were other ways of saying it, which would have been much more welcoming:

'May I see your ticket, please?'

or

'Good morning, sir. May I see your ticket? Thank you.'

The bloke might as well have held out his hand and said,

'Ticket. You do not have to say anything, but it may harm your defence if you do not mention when questioned something which you later rely on in court'.

The two words he'd spoken didn't deserve even one in response. From my pocket, I took the ticket I had purchased the day before and handed it to the bouncer. I didn't receive any thanks, nor did I expect any. Heaven help me if I had been ticketless. He might have manhandled me, shackled me to one of his cronies and had me carted off to a dusty office on the station to await trial.

Thankfully, my Travelcard passed inspection. I was going to see Wayne and Sara. Mama Vida was going to be there, too, and I was looking forward to seeing them all.

*****

I have come through my first year without you and I can't help thinking that my gallivanting – visiting and meeting up with people I haven't seen in years – has been my opportunity to say goodbye to those who know me.

I was never the life and soul. That was your forte. But I have hooked up with old school friends, people abroad, former work colleagues, nurses and your family, all as I have never done in the past; as we never even did as a couple.

The feeling I have is that magical, mystical forces are at work, preparing those around me for the time when I come to join you. I'm not ill though, at least, not physically ill. I often think I might have bowel cancer, or liver disease, or some other horrible condition that has taken my muscle tone away, caused me to lose weight and left me wondering if the hard lump in my abdomen is a growth. I wonder too if the pain I sometimes have in my head, the sudden bouts of tiredness and the forgetfulness are a result of a brain tumour. For all that, I'm still here and none of my symptoms is worthy of a trip to the doctor. I just keep thinking that I'm 'being prepared' in some way and that those who know me will have at least seen me before I go.

And that's fine, as long as I can be given something for the pain, if and when it comes. To be with you is a thought that comes to me almost every single day of the life left in me. And every day that passes brings me a little closer to the one that will be my last.

This is not how I should live and it's not how I should die. These are obviously still dark days for me. I cannot see what lies beyond because I can't find the means to light my way.

*****

I wanted to go back to the Day Therapy Unit at the West Berkshire Community Hospital today. You and I went there often enough that we formed friendships with other cancer patients and with staff. I've been preparing extracts from *Bright Lights and Fairy Dust* with accompanying letters asking for consent. I wanted to write as many letters as possible that could be left there, but it came down to just three addressees in the end: everyone at the Day Therapy Unit, the Occupational Health Consultant and the Palliative Care Consultant. It has involved a great deal of work and I was still busy preparing text this morning. As a result, it was after midday when I eventually got to the Day Therapy Unit.

My timing was good though, because the Palliative Care Consultant was there. We talked for at least ten minutes and I was able to hand over in person the text blocks I'd spent days putting together. The wad of paper was at least an inch thick.

I look forward to hearing from him in due course but, because there's so much there, I realise it might be a while before I hear back.

*****

Perhaps not everyone will agree, but I think we're having a beautiful autumn this year. Although there has already been plenty of leaf fall, many trees still have brightly coloured leaves on them and as I travelled to London on the train with my sister Linda this morning, we looked out at some stunning colours. Deep reds; bright yellows; warm oranges.

While we were in London, Wayne took us for a stroll around what is known as 'The Conservation Area' and Telegraph Hill. In one of the parks there, I sloshed my way through a thick carpet of yellow leaves beneath a big old plane tree. Doing so reminded me again of days in primary school, when it wasn't enough to see what was happening in nature at this time of year.

We were allowed outside to experience it. We would pile autumn leaves high and wade through them, or crawl under them, or leave a pile somewhere for hedgehogs to hibernate and keep warm under during the winter. We would also collect different fallen leaves and take them indoors, where some were painted with poster paints and used like block prints on paper while others were dried slowly until only their veins remained. The beauty of Nature has never been lost on me.

*****

I've seen you twice this week, my Darling.

The first time was as I drove to the Day Therapy Unit on Wednesday. You were walking with another lady on The Green. And now today, when I cycled back from town this afternoon, I caught sight of you in the Market Place. You were window shopping.

These were fleeting glimpses seen in the faces and shapes of other women. I think this is the first time, since you went away just over a year ago, that this phenomenon has occurred, and I wonder, '*Why?*'

I wonder, too, what the analysts, psychologists and clinicians would make of it in itself, as well as the timing of it.

The emotions associated with these sightings were, on both occasions, mixed. On the one hand I had a jolt of adrenaline, like an electric shock, when at first I thought it *was* you. It was a buzz, but it lasted only seconds. Then I felt my heart was heavy again and I was sad because I knew it wasn't true.

*****

I sent an email to The Enchanted Manor, to let Ric and Maggie know that the twins will soon be here. I'm sure you would like me to tell them, especially since they have met Wayne and Sara now. I told them Sara is booked on Monday for an elected Caesarian.

No one here knows what they're having and they haven't let anyone know the names they've chosen, so I promised I would let Ric and Maggie know in the coming days and send them another email. I will attach a photo when I do.

Ric and Maggie returned enchanted wishes and they are looking forward to hearing all about the happy event.

*****

Dressed in a thick, felt coat, I was crouched, frog-like, at the end of your plot. Surrounded by the beauty of autumn colour I noticed the faintest trace of rain in the air: a *smirr* so light that it felt as though it wouldn't even hit the ground. But it did, and this I knew because I reached out to your stone and it was damp to the touch. Not wet, but damp, and peppered with what appeared to be young lichens starting to grow on the Portland stone. Once again Acorn Ridge afforded me beauty in every direction, in spite of the drab weather.

The words on your stone, although they were upside down from my current viewpoint, were perfectly clear. I read them; thought about the past year. It just wasn't fair.

'Well, Darling,' I started to talk quietly to you, 'tomorrow's the big day. The twins are arriving. Oh, how I wish that you were here with me. It breaks my heart that you won't see them. I know how overjoyed you would be.'

Not only is it unfair that you should have left us so soon at all, but the fact that you had to endure a harsh illness fills me with abiding sadness. And nor is it fair that we were parted. You were my life.

'I love you,' I said, taking my fingertips off your stone as I stood up.

Momentarily standing sentinel at your graveside I suddenly heard the sound of voices behind me and I turned to see four people striding out across the grass to a plot further down the hill from yours. Another bereavement. Their presence interrupted my peace and my thoughts and so I decided to leave. I checked that autumn was having the right effect on what remained of your hawthorn tree. It seemed to be, so I turned and walked back across the grass to the car.

'I'll bring you some photos,' I whispered, 'so you can see the babies. I'll be back in a couple of days, Dolly.'

Just as I reached the car I looked down and saw a small, white feather on the ground.

I believe.

And I believe you know exactly what's happening back here.

*****

At around 6.40 a.m. I sent Wayne and Sara a text. It read, simply, 'xxxx'.

Moments later they returned the sentiment by texting two kisses back. They were on the way to the hospital for the planned delivery by Caesarian.

Not long after, I walked to the supermarket to get some milk. I'd also gone to get flowers for you and some 6 x 4 photo paper so that I would be able to print pictures of the babies and take them to Acorn Ridge as promised.

I couldn't tell what the weather was going to do. Dark clouds filled the sky, backlit by low autumn sun, and it looked as if it might even rain. But when I came out of the supermarket, it was a Wagamama day! I'm sure you moved those clouds on just for us. The sky was blue and the morning was now bathed in sunshine. It was a beautiful day on which to welcome newcomers to the world. Tears filled my eyes on the way home, although they didn't fall. They were the tears of one desperately sad that his Darling wife wasn't with him to share the moment.

I kept busy throughout the morning. I finally painted the lounge and kitchen doors with the top coat of 'Cream White' that I'd bought months earlier. It was satisfying to know that I was on the way to completing a long overdue job.

Except that I didn't quite finish it, because Wayne called not long after midday.

'What do you think?' he asked.

'A boy and a girl, I reckon,' I replied, itching to know the outcome.

'Two girls.' As he told me he chuckled, and I could visualise the broadest smile on Wayne's face as he continued to tell me about them. 'Lola Vida, 7lb 4oz, and Darcy Linda, 6lb 6oz, born at 1005. Everything's fine. You're my first call.'

It was fantastic news.

My own Dad was then my first call.

During the rest of the day, the news rippled across this country and abroad.

Our grandchildren have arrived!

*****

Wayne sent me some photos of the twins and at home I printed one off on the paper I'd bought the day before. On the back of it I wrote, 'My Darling Linda, meet Lola and Darcy. Thank you. I love you'. I signed it with that special heart and arrow thing we used to share and I placed it in a plastic pouch.

I also wrote a short poem:

> *'Welcome to the world'*
> *Says Grandpa to his girls,*
> *'May your childhoods be playful*
> *And your lives ever joyful.*
> *But, most of all, please know,*
> *That wherever you go,*
> *And all else above,*
> *You shall always have love'.*

I drove up to Acorn Ridge that morning.

I thought I'd feel differently. I thought I'd be bouncing, like the cat I accidently trapped in our greenhouse a few weeks ago. Instead, I feel only sadness that you aren't here to share the moment. This grandparent thing should be a joint experience. Doing it on my own makes it feel like only half the fun.

I am happy, but I seem to be happy without the smiles. I am happy on the inside that everything worked out okay. The girls are fine. Sara, although she is suffering pain from the Caesarian, is fine. Wayne is shattered, but fine. They have a family now. Our family has grown a bit but you aren't – can't be – here, to physically be part of it.

It doesn't seem to matter what anyone says, I can only see the situation my way. My joy is offset by my grief, which appears to be the heavier of the two emotions.

I hope, as time goes on, that I will feel differently.

*****

With my Mum and my sister, Linda, I went to meet Lola and Darcy for the first time today. The little ladies are still in hospital with Sara. Everything's fine, Darling, don't worry. Sara is exhausted – and I'm not surprised – but she and Wayne are very proud parents.

The twins don't look alike. We've always known that would be the case. Linda, they are so tiny, so fragile. I am in awe when I think how Sara has been carrying these little bundles of love all this time. And although they're not identical, I'm going to have to pay attention to put the right name to the right granddaughter. Lola's got a bit more hair than Darcy and I'm sure that will help me in that regard.

Wayne and I took a coffee break, downstairs, and he asked what the girls should call me as they grow up. I'd already decided I was a Grandpa, not a Granddad. I added Wayne's word for me.

'I'm going to be Grandpa Pops,' I said.

His approving smile lit up the coffee bar.

And you, my Darling, will be their 'Nanny Linda'.

*****

The next day, I went back to Purley-on-Thames. The Bereavement Group hadn't met for two weeks and the consensus was that we had missed our meeting. I know

I had, even though I'd been busy for the past two weeks with London, painting doors, the Day Therapy Unit and two new granddaughters.

It was different there today, but in a positive way. I saw connections being made within the group. There was the touching of hands, the squeezing of same. I saw encouragement *of* group members *by* group members, without, it seemed to me, the need to route it through the actual session. That was during the halfway coffee break.

I got a sense that some of the members of the group are now stronger than they were when we began five weeks earlier. They may not think so, but I reckon that's what I saw today. In that context, I believe that we have all derived something positive from our meetings and our talking. Whilst nothing can take away the pain we feel, we have admitted that we like our little group. We like it because we all have something in common and we can talk openly and honestly about how we feel instead of having to button up because it's been a while since our partners died. Some in the group have admitted that friends, and even family, have 'moved on' since the death and they either expect or hope that we have too. But ours is a different grief to theirs.

That's one of the reasons why the group is important, because for its members our grief is similar, familiar, sustained, ongoing, and recognisable. Our emotions can be shared without judgment or prejudice. No one in the group would dream of suggesting to another that they should 'snap out of it'.

I feel that I am being treated for my grief and I feel that the treatment is helping me.

*****

There were several cars in the car park at Acorn Ridge today, but I didn't see anyone I knew and I don't think the different groups of people I saw were connected. They were, just like me, simply visiting. I stood for a long time at your side and tried to ignore the others, but it was difficult.

I didn't say much to you, but I thought a lot. I thought of our grandchildren. I also thought about what's going on here and what will happen at Acorn Ridge over the coming years. There are more graves than when I was here last. This is evident by the stack of flowers over a cremation spot and a pile of freshly dug earth on top of a burial.

I walked around; checked on some people we knew; saw 'new' neighbours. One, recently buried, was a twelve year old boy. What had happened, I wondered: accident or illness?

12 is no age.

Mind you, neither is 57.

Back at your grave, I reached down with my fingertips.

'I'll see you, Darling,' I whispered, hoping I would feel a little less distracted next time.

*****

I feel as though I've lost my way a bit. For the past couple of days I haven't been able to concentrate.

I'm adrift.

I can do stuff – I *do* do stuff – but I think a little bit of the spark has gone from me.

It might be that I am worrying again. I worry that I don't have a job and, although I want one, I'm concerned that I might have to settle for something I don't really want to do. Christmas is looming, too and that's probably got a lot to do with it. I want to run away from it, but there can be no escape. How is Christmas going to go for me this year?

*****

When I woke the next morning I felt altogether different. A new day, a new approach.

Did you do something to me?

Something had definitely happened, because I knew I was much more upbeat.

Perhaps a chemical imbalance was put right.

*****

She was wearing your black coat – the one you bought from Wallis. The lady on the train was in the seat in front of me. She had your black mohair hat on, too. And your ears, she had your ears. They reminded me of when I met you all those years ago, when you wore your hair short.

I couldn't see her face, but it didn't matter. The lovely thing was that it was like having you near me, even though I wasn't able speak to you. I was also surprised it didn't upset me. I felt that you were close and it gladdened my heart.

Our granddaughters are beautiful, Darling. Darcy is a bit smaller than Lola, but both of them are lively and vocal and they both feed well. They're both so tiny. To hold their new lives in my hands makes me very proud and I know beyond doubt that you would be absolutely delighted to meet them and happy, of course, for Wayne and Sara. It's taken them a long time and it hasn't been easy. I am thrilled that our family has grown.

I had a relaxing day with them and with Wayne, Sara and Mama Vida.

*****

It was our nephew Jason's seventh birthday. Timing my visit so that it would coincide with his return from school, I walked across town to give him his present: watercolour paper and paints. On the way, the weather fell apart and it was raining steadily by the time I got there. As four o'clock approached, my Mum arrived in her car and gave Jason his present from Nan and Grandad: drawing paper and pencils. A theme was evident.

Mum offered to take me home but I said I wanted to go to the wood yard, so she dropped me off nearby. It saved me getting too wet, for the rain by now was persistent. As I walked into the wood yard, I realised it had been a while since I had been there and for a moment I didn't know – couldn't think – what to do. Then I remembered that I should select the wood first and get a yard ticket.

I waited a very long time to be served in the yard. In the end, I selected my own timber and cut it so that I could carry it home. One of the staff gave me a yard ticket, which I took into the shop. It was quite a lot of money for not a lot of wood and it was only when I went to pay that I remembered I also had a trade card.

I asked the chap behind the counter if the trade card would still be valid, as I hadn't used it for a very long time. With patience, he cancelled everything he had just input and did it all again. I got forty percent off, which made a big saving. He told me I had last used it in spring last year.

Having someone force me to think back to last year came as a bit of a shock.

'I knew it had been a while,' I said, pondering, as the words left my mouth, on just what was going on in March last year.

So, eighteen months, I thought. I must have been doing something to the house. But what? One thing was certain: in March last year I still had you, my Darling, and you were still getting about. I would not have done woodwork otherwise.

When I got home and checked, I found that last year the supplier had delivered three interior doors to us. These were the doors I pledged to you that I would fit, so that you could see the house finished.

I fitted them, but I left them unpainted.

*****

It was cold last night. I went to the Newbury Chamber Choir *Rossetti Requiem* and Mozart concert at the church. Afterwards, when I came out of the church to go home, it was so cold that I thought it was freezing.

When I looked out this morning though, there wasn't any frost. It was just a dull, gloomy and foggy November morning.

At Acorn Ridge, the fog shrouded the hills and it was only just possible to see the edge of the site. I looked up and there seemed to be a hole in the sky and I thought I could see the making of a Wagamama day ahead. It was only just after nine, so it was possible, after all, that the day might improve.

There didn't seem to be much to cheer me about your resting place today, but then I spotted the tip of one of the crocus bulbs, then another and another. They are already trying to peep through.

One of Christina Rossetti's poems from last night's concert suddenly came into my head. I don't mean that I could recite it, Darling, just that I remembered enough of it to want to re-read it from last night's programme when I got home.

Remember Me

Remember me when I am gone away,
Gone far away into the silent land;
When you can no more hold me by the hand,
Nor I half turn to go yet turning stay.
Remember me when no more day by day.
You tell me of our future that you plann'd:
Only remember me; you understand
It will be late to counsel then or pray.
Yet if you should forget me for a while
And afterwards remember, do not grieve:
For if the darkness and corruption leave
A vestige of the thoughts that once I had,
Better by far you should forget and smile
Than that you should remember and be sad

*****

It was the last Bereavement Group session today and we returned evaluation forms that we'd been given the previous week. Linda, I must tell you I have found the sessions helpful to my healing and I am grateful not only to the Duchess of Kent Hospice and the facilitators, but to every member of our group. We may still hurt – may never fully recover – but, speaking for myself, I think the whole experience has strengthened and encouraged me.

In preparation for this, our final session, we had also been asked to bring in something to eat so that we could share lunch. Group members brought in sandwiches, snacks, cake. Me? I baked a cheese and lentil gratin, something you and I often made from the recipe in our little vegetarian cookbook. There was friendly conversation among us all. There was laughter; understanding; empathy. We were connected.

Before the session concluded, our group talked about meeting again, just the ten of us.

*****

To anyone watching from across the valley, it must have looked very odd indeed to see a man inspecting one of the plots at Acorn Ridge with such a close eye. He was wearing bicycle clips; he was bending forwards over the mound, his face only inches away from the grass on top. Straightening his posture, he then sidestepped a few inches before thrusting his face down again.

That particular plot was yours and the man – of course – was me.

It snowed that morning. There wasn't a lot and the flakes were so tiny that all they had done was lightly coat everything in a white crust, like a dusting of icing sugar. I had chosen to cycle to Acorn Ridge. For one thing I needed the exercise, but it was also the Hennessy Gold Cup at Newbury Racecourse, so traffic would be bad as the day stretched out.

What was I doing?

Just checking your crocuses again.

The band played a charity ceilidh in Kintbury in the evening. When we loaded our cars afterwards I couldn't help noticing how big the moon was. It was cut off at the top but otherwise enormous and golden in colour, its features softened by a mist that put it out of focus. It was low and in the east, so I drove towards it almost all the way home. I didn't notice it getting any bigger, even after five miles, but the moon certainly impressed me that night.

*****

Another rant, Darling:

I have a deep loathing of *those* Christmas songs, which play every year in shops and malls. You know the ones I mean. They're the same songs that we have had to listen to for decades. I wonder annually what people get out of them, apart from the artists receiving their royalties. I can tolerate them at low volume. However, when I have them blasted into my ear I want to flee and, lately, I have done just that.

Earlier this week, I went looking for an outfit for one of our grandchildren and wandered into one of the town's department stores. I took the assault on my ears for as long as I could but had to run away after three songs. Honestly, Dolly, it was torture. This morning a do-it-yourself store, normally careful not to blast the customer's ears, disappointed me. I stood in the gardening section listening briefly to lyrics that told me it was going to be a sad Christmas without you. 'Bloody right', I muttered aloud before moving on in haste. The final straw this morning came when I walked into a large shop selling everything to do with babies and toddlers. I was still hoping to buy an outfit similar to the one you had bought last year when we thought we might become grandparents to one child. That outfit is at home, still in the memory box you left for us.

I managed only a glance at three sets of children's clothing before I had to walk out.

*****

I woke up to the clock radio and listened to the news and weather. Snow had spread right across the country, in varying degrees of thickness. When I got up and went downstairs, I saw that we'd had at least half an inch. It was a thicker dusting than we'd had four days ago and it looked pretty. It looked 'Christmassy'.

Gosh, I cannot think when we have had snow at this time of year.

*****

In the past week we have had snow, ice and rain. And now, today, we have clear blue sky. It's a Wagamama day and I have come to your plot again. It's cold. The temperature gauge in the car tells me it is four degrees outside. The sun is low, even though it's two in the afternoon. It won't be long before it gives up here and hurries off to greet someone else for their new day.

Last week Abi, who makes her own jewellery, gave me a glass crystal to put up here for you. It's round, about 50mm across and quite heavy, too. It was in a little decorative bag with a note of support and encouragement.

I hung it on your hawthorn tree today and straight away the sunbeams bounced off it, peppering the ground with a spectrum of glitter.

Not much else has changed really. The grass hasn't grown and the bulb shoots are no bigger than the last time I was here. But they will be.

The other thing that hasn't changed is my love for you.

I miss you, Darling.

*****

It was less than two weeks ago that our 'official' Bereavement Group met for the last time. Today, we followed up on our pledge to meet as a group on our own.

I collected Dennis from his home, as it was on my way, and drove to Calcot. The small hotel was central for us all and turned out to be a good meeting place. We ordered coffee and biscuits and had the lounge area pretty much to ourselves. Conversation felt relaxed and our little group went on for an hour and a half.

Before leaving, we set a date early in the New Year to do this again.

Later that day I popped into town to post my overseas Christmas cards and to purchase an oil-filled radiator for Wayne and Sara for Christmas. Their bathroom is freezing.

I thought I would try my luck at picking up a cheap sweater from a charity shop. And I might have done, had any of them had something that fitted me. I went into three of them on my way to the Post Office, all to no avail. Then, on the way to buy the radiator, I went into one of the charity shops on the west side of the Mall. I was thumbing through the very small selection of oversized jumpers and fleeces there when I heard someone behind me asking a question.

'How much is that Rottweiler in the window?'

I couldn't believe that I'd heard someone genuinely inquiring as to the price of a 'doggie in the window'. It was a question that had been asked over fifty years earlier by a singer whose surname matches mine – Patti Page – and I couldn't help but smile at the woollens before turning to leave.

By then the shop assistant and the customer were at the front of the shop, where a very large and cuddly, stuffed toy Rottweiler had been plucked from the window display. It was being rotated into several positions, none of which a Rottweiler would ever permit and none of which appeared to produce the answer to the question that had been asked. On that basis, if there was to be a sale, the shop assistant would have to take the lead, because the customer was probably trying to sniff out a bargain.

*****

Christmas came; my second without you, my Love. And once again I could not bear to spend it at home. I had to get away and get through it on my own terms.

There was snow on the ground and it was bitterly cold. Online, I had found a Bed & Breakfast about a forty minute drive north. It was far enough away that I could feel it was a break, but I also knew I could pull out at any time if everything came crashing down on me or if the weather worsened. When I called the B&B to book, I was pleased to hear the landlady, Sarah, say they weren't doing Christmas because their daughter was away at university. Their celebrations would start in a few days when she came home. I couldn't help wondering if you had helped me find this place, because it sounded over the phone like exactly what I wanted.

That evening, I sat down to dinner in the farmhouse kitchen. Sarah had provided a light meal, just for me it seemed, and she joined me at the old pine table.

'So what brings you to a place like this at Christmas?' she asked. 'Shouldn't you be with family?' A moment passed. 'Have you got family?'

I thought I'd get straight to it. 'I'm widowed', I replied.

'I knew it!' She gave me a little smile and pushed herself back from the table slightly. 'I knew when I spoke to you on the phone. And you want to get away from Christmas.'

I raised my eyebrows and nodded in agreement as I picked at the last of my meal. Our conversation from then on was comfortable and we sat at the table for nearly an hour, just chatting. This was what I needed, above sympathy and avoiding my bereavement.

*****

I turned the key in the car on Christmas Eve morning. The temperature gauge indicated that it was minus one outside. With such low temperatures having lasted for several days, it was therefore small wonder that the snow had not melted. It was a white Christmas in West Challow, near Wantage. The surroundings appeared to be sparsely populated and the Downland to the south and the Vale of the White Horse in the north were heavy with snow. It was treacherous and for some perhaps unwelcome, but it was also extremely pretty.

Sarah had asked me during dinner last night what I would be doing today. I told her I planned to go into Wantage. I didn't tell her I was hoping to find a tattoo parlour because I wanted my navel re-pierced for Christmas, but I did suggest that I would pop into any charity shops in the town. She had told me there was an excellent museum and I made a mental note of that. I told her I hoped to attend a midnight mass on Christmas Eve and I knew that St. Peter and St. Paul in Wantage had one at 11.30pm. She told me that the local church also had one. It was closer and she said that she would speak to her friend, whom she thought would probably be attending, and let me know today.

I popped my head round the kitchen door before leaving the house and asked Sarah about the mass tonight. She and her friend were going and Sarah offered to take me to the church at Childrey.

As the engine ticked over and I let the car warm up, I considered my plans for the day. I would drive into Wantage to look around; spend as long as I could there. However, I thought I would start by driving to Childrey and get an understanding of where the village is and what the church is like.

I set off a little after 9.00 a.m. and located St.Mary's church at the end of a snow-packed cul-de-sac. The absence of grit salt and regular traffic had resulted in the road being almost untouched. There was only space for about four cars at the end of the road, so I imagined that parking later would be a bit awkward. I took a couple of photographs before heading into Wantage.

I parked on ice in an otherwise slushy car park and paid £1.00 for three hours. That was very good value. As I walked through to the town, I saw that there was a busy market in the town centre, a special one for Christmas perhaps. I went into lots of charity shops looking for bargains and then came across the old Regent. Once a cinema, this was now a second-hand bookshop. I bought two books from the vast collection there. My purchase made no dint in the stock levels, but I was happy with what I'd picked up.

I found the museum and spent a long time there going through the many exhibits before enjoying a mocha coffee and portion of fruit crumble in the museum's cafe.

When I got back to the Bed and Breakfast in the afternoon, my navel was still intact, so I'll try to change that next week, but I'd had an interesting time anyway. I retired to my room until 11.00 p.m. at which time, exactly as instructed earlier that morning, I went downstairs to find Sarah.

In the kitchen, three young women sat around the big pine table. Sarah wasn't one of them.

'She's gone to put an extra jumper on,' one of them said.

'Is it that cold out then?' I asked.

'It is in the church,' a different woman replied.

Moments later, Sarah came in.

'I just need to put my boots on and we'll go', she said. 'We'll take the truck because the hill's too icy for the car. I tried earlier and had to turn back - the car just wouldn't get up there.'

Looking frantically for the truck keys, Sarah went into their living room to ask the men if they knew where the keys might be. She emerged with the keys and her son, who had decided in that moment that he wanted to come to the midnight mass with us.

As we left the farm, driving away beneath a clear and starlit sky, I saw what Sarah meant when she'd said the hill was too icy. But the Mazda pickup took it in its stride. Her friend was waiting at the side of the road in Childrey and we pulled up next to her. Moments later, we arrived at the church. The road, white and shiny, almost luminescent with packed ice, did not offer much in the way of parking, so Sarah put the vehicle up on a snow-covered grass bank and we decamped, as though abandoning the vehicle.

The women had been right: it was cold inside the church. Members of the congregation were channelled into enclosed pews and as soon as each row was full, a small door was closed. I don't know if I imagined it, but it seemed to me that closing the door kept in some of our body heat.

It was a great service and some young farmers at the back of the church belted out the hymns. Their presence impressed Sarah's son, who was glad he had come along.

This was my second midnight mass without you, but you are always in my heart and I felt you were with me. Once again, just as I had at last year's midnight mass in Wales, I went to the altar rail for a blessing. Sarah later asked if I had ever considered being confirmed so that I could take communion, to which I replied that it was something I have been thinking about for a very long time.

'Will you do something for me?' she asked. 'If you do get confirmed, will you let me know? I'd like to be there.'

I was touched by her friendly and encouraging personality and promised I would. And I felt blessed once again to have met some lovely people there in Oxfordshire.

*****

On Christmas Day, on my way to the dining room, I stepped outside the open front door of the Bed and Breakfast. I was dressed only in trousers and a shirt. The sun was rising above the downs; the sky was deep blue, the morning cold and crisp. I picked up snow with un-gloved hands and formed balls to throw for Daisy and Molly, who pranced and scampered around as though they'd never seen it before.

I was reminded of our own spaniel, Burma. He loved snow, but when it turned into little ice balls between his phalanges it made him hobble.

It was a Wagamama day! After breakfast I dressed up against the weather and went out on my walk. As I trudged across the winter landscape leaving behind me the pattern of my walking boots in the crunching snow, my mobile rang. I pulled off one of my gloves and took the call from Wayne and Sara. They sent me Christmas blessings and thanks. I returned the sentiments and explained that I was heading up to The Ridgeway for a long walk.

It was beautiful up there and the views were spectacular, but I had to keep alert to the terrain and the ice and snow. I'm not sure that I could have done many more miles. Trying to maintain my grip on the icier sections was especially tiring on my legs. By the time I approached my lodgings the sun was sinking fast and I was glad I hadn't left it any later.

Although I had enjoyed my day on the hills, I missed coming home and sharing my experience with you.

*****

On Boxing Day, I set off North for the Cotswolds. Our friends, Tony and Maria, had hired a cottage in Bibury over Christmas and invited me to join them for the day. There was still a great deal of snow around and, in places, ice that seemed diamond-hard across some of the lanes. When I got there, without incident I am happy to say, I saw the village as a living Christmas Card and the beauty of my surroundings was a genuine tonic. I went walking with Tony and Ruby, the dog, and wondered why I had never visited the village before.

I shared the rest of the day, and a very fine meal, with Tony, Maria and their family, before driving home.

I returned to the reality of my situation.

Three

H ello, Darling.

It's almost the end of January. I haven't written to you for nearly a month! That's terrible. Is this another indication that I have 'moved forward'; 'moved on'? (Dare I use these phrases?) Or, is it that I'm just lazy? Maybe I haven't written because there's been nothing new to tell you. I didn't even celebrate New Year.

After seeing the family at the usual Sunday morning gathering at number thirty, I went up to Acorn Ridge today. It was cold and grey. A biting wind tried to force its way through my thick coat, but I had wrapped up well and was warm. Everything at your plot is trying to grow, but those pesky rabbits have been munching on your crocus leaves. How do I stop that?

*****

I ran my fingers across your photograph as I considered swapping it out of its frame. I thought I might put one of us, taken at Speen Church during our walk to Donnington two years ago, in its place. Then I began to talk to your picture.

'I've got all this.' I looked around before continuing. 'The house, a pension. But I have nothing. I am... nothing... without you. I miss you, baby. I miss you so much. I love you, Linda.'

Oh, Darling, it hurts me that you cannot enjoy our grandchildren as I am doing.

*****

I have been agonising over my current feelings, which scream to me that they are different even from what they were a month ago. As my sister, Linda, put it, 'You are in that frame of mind'.

And so I am. I am ready to take another step forward and engage in romance. I hope you understand, Darling, and that you don't mind. I know, though, that my bereavement makes me vulnerable and I must be careful.

I will be careful.

Promise.

*****

When I got home and opened the front door, I saw a business flyer on the floor. I get a lot of these and I always admire those individuals who go to the time and effort of producing advertising material and then go round posting it to drum up business. All sorts of flyers have plopped on to the doormat over the years. Quite apart from those that have been delivered by almost every exotic restaurant in the town, I have received blurb from plumbers, window cleaners, a chimney sweep, handymen, an oven-cleaning service, persons who 'iron by weight', house cleaners, tree surgeons, landscape gardeners, house clearance specialists and estate agents. *'No job too small'. 'We're currently in your street'. 'Same-day service'. 'Free delivery'.* I thought I'd had the full range until today, because I had never had a business flyer that offered 'hovering' and 'moping' to customers. As soon as I read the flyer, and I always read every one, a little chuckle slipped from my mouth.

'I can do that for myself,' I mumbled aloud.

I finished reading the rest of the flyer. It came from a couple who offered a friendly cleaning service in the area. I don't know why, but I thought I could help their business by interrupting their print run and having the typos corrected.

I prepared a short text on my mobile and sent it to the number on the flyer:

'No need of your services, thank you, but you should change some spelling.

It should read Hoovering and Mopping.'

A little later, I received a text in response.

'Thank you for letting me know. Regards, Agnes.'

I felt pleased that I was able to help.

I have never heard anything else from them, but I hope they're doing okay and not moping too much.

*****

'At that point you knew your life was everything it could be.'

I woke up at five o'clock this morning and these words, in this order, were inside my head. They were so clear and strong that I went downstairs and, on the way to the bathroom, took a pen from the kitchen drawer and wrote them down. I went back to bed and fell asleep.

When I woke again at 6.30 I could not remember the words – not all of them anyway. I read them from the scrap of paper I had used.

Where did they come from and what did they mean?

*****

It was late when I got home. I saw that the answering machine was flashing. I played it back. Dad wanted to tell me how he had got on with the specialist the day before. I would have to ring him in the morning now, so I added him to the list of people I had to contact, but I put him at the top of the list.

*****

Dad beat me to it and called me at 9.45 a.m.

The consultant had not liked the look of Dad's ulcerated leg when he saw it. Swabs were taken for analysis and Dad will be weaned off the warfarin (anticoagulant) for a short time, so that a biopsy can be taken from the messy wound. He has a follow-up appointment with his GP next Tuesday.

'They think it might be C,' Dad said.

'It's taken them three months to see you, but now it's an emergency?' I was cross with the system. 'It doesn't surprise me though, Pa. Remember last year, I thought it was cancer then. It's a shame it's taken them so long to come up with a potential diagnosis.'

*****

I spent a weekend with our friends in Lymington. You know how Ian and I used to walk miles together. He wanted to introduce me to another long distance path, although we would only take in part of it. The Solent Way is a 60 mile path that runs from Milford-on-Sea to Emsworth and it takes in a little of the New Forest. I just want to tell you about something that happened to us on a section between Lymington and Beaulieu.

As Ian and I came out of the woods, we saw a New Forest pony sitting on the grass ahead, looking like a dog stretched out on a hearth rug. We got closer and the pony pulled itself up into a standing position. It didn't run off, but stood there, eyeing us, perhaps trying to decide whether or not we posed a threat. I made that *'cack, cack'* noise that horse owners make when they are attracting the attention of their animals. The pony's ears pricked up and angled in our direction. It ambled over to us. For a few minutes, Ian and I just studied the animal. Its coat was long and dark, but patchy across its back. Perhaps it had nibbled itself there, or maybe other horses had taken chunks of hair.

I remembered that Kathy had put a packet of dried apricots in my backpack. Against all the rules, I decided to try offering the pony a piece of dried fruit. I placed an apricot on the palm of my hand, tucked my thumb tightly against the side of my forefinger and held out my hand like a flat plate. With caution the pony took a small step forward. It craned its neck, but a further step in our direction was required to reach the apricot. The pony moved closer and put its nose to my hand, sniffing at the orange-coloured disc in my palm at the same time wobbling its tough lips – even daring to let them touch the tips of my fingers. I had to be careful that the pony didn't bite me. When at last it took the apricot it gave us a nod of approval.

'Another one?' I asked.

I placed a second apricot in my hand and held it out. Carefully, again it took it from me. I had just two more pieces of fruit left and gave them both to the animal. Still we could not get so close as to be able to stroke it. We walked away; the pony followed. We stopped; the pony stopped.

'I haven't got anymore.'

We began to walk off again, the pony followed. We had made a friend with a taste for dried apricots.

*****

It was just before eight in the morning, on a perfect Wagamama day, when I set off north to attend the funeral of Dan, our friend's son. We had met him a few times when visiting Lyn.

After a freezing night, it was a stunning morning. The sun, still rising into a cloudless sky, had so far burned off all the frost it could reach. As I drove along the motorway, I could see areas in the shadow of trees and hills that were still waiting for its touch. Above them, the white vapour trails of busy air traffic stood out against the deep blue of a late winter sky.

Oh, Darling, how sad that Dan took his own life. He was a troubled man who was too young to die, but he must have felt that he wasn't able to stay. He was a tormented soul who has left family and friends shocked and bereft. Lyn's ex-husband had died only a few weeks ago. Now, her son was in a coffin.

The funeral service moved me. The crematorium chapel was packed to capacity and several people had to stand in the aisle.

As well as paying my respects to Dan, I had gone to support Lyn at what can only be a terrible time in her life. She helped Brenda and David and she was there for you and me when you battled against your cancer. I wanted to be there for her at this awful time, something you and I would have done together without a second thought.

After the service, there was a reception. Tea and sandwiches, in the British Legion, the same place that we had Brenda's. Memories came flooding back once again. I thought about Brenda's stoicism, about David's resignation and I thought again about your strength.

*****

Dennis said a strange thing today, when I took him home. We had been to our monthly meeting in Calcot with the rest of the group.

Dennis is 82 years old and his wife, Betty, died around the same time as you. He considers himself to be 'in God's waiting room' and it is a sad truth that he is not enjoying good health. However, none of this set me thinking that what he said was strange. No, it was when the moment came that I dropped him off at his bungalow and he said he would step indoors and his only greeting was going to be from his cat. He'd got the cat from the adoption centre a few months earlier and wouldn't be without it now. Although I have never liked cats, I have seen the bond these two have developed. The one needs the other.

'But it's not the same is it, going back to a cat?' It was more of a statement than a question. He continued to apprise me of his thoughts. 'There was a time when you'd get home and your wife would say, *How did you get on, Love?'*

Sorry, Linda, but that sent my mind into a loop, because if she were to say that to him, or if you said it to me, then Dennis and I wouldn't be attending our bereavement group coffee morning.

*****

As far as I remember, the last time I had this 'asthma' – if that's what it is – was when you were dying. It continued for weeks after you left us and was a real nuisance.

I had noticed something of a cough coming on the day after we played the St. Patrick's Day engagement. I wondered if I'd picked something up there. In equal measure, I wondered if something was already brewing, even before our performance. Anyway, the upshot is that this ridiculous cough has got a little worse every day. When it kicks off I can feel my air passages tightening. The more I try to suppress my coughing, the worse it gets. I've had to get my inhaler out and start using it to reduce the constriction. And my stomach hurts now, with all the coughing. I can see how a person could easily get a hernia by coughing.

It is painful to swallow and if it doesn't improve by next week I think I might have to ask the doctor for some help.

I was on a steam inhalation at three o'clock this morning, which I think has helped.

*****

I was at the home of Kip and Nina, hosts that evening to the Lent course that some of us are doing. When the course leader had first asked me to join, some weeks ago now, I declined because I wasn't sure if I could commit. He'd asked me again a couple of weeks later and I put my name down.

'I'll see where it takes me,' I said.

I didn't know how it would go. It's been a while since I got this close to religion and the bible.

We were asked to consider our faith and what it means to us. Some of us were in pairs, while others were in groups, and we exchanged views on the subject. One of the points was around discussing our faith with others. I said that I tend not to do that because whenever I mention in the slightest anything to do with church, the usual response is 'Well, Chris, if that's what gives you comfort'.

It's not that at all. I go to church to gain a deeper understanding of everything that has happened to you and to me. Does theism help? I think it does, but I don't know enough and probably never will. I'm willing to keep asking, searching. Does believing in God mean I can't believe in a spiritual world? I hope not, because I continue to draw strength from my thoughts around sunbeams, butterflies and feathers.

The course leader suggested that the many stories in the books of the bible show us facets of religion, of faith. He said we don't see the entire jewel, just the facets of the gem glinting at us from time to time. I'd never thought of it in those terms, but I locked on to his comments and they made sense to me.

I wanted to say (but didn't, in case it was an obvious thing to think) that I could relate to the analogy and that I hoped at the end, when my time comes to join you, I will be able to see the entire jewel and everything will be right.

*****

Dad had his biopsy today and I rang him tonight to ask how he had got on. He said the doctor had made a series of incisions (after injecting a local anaesthetic, of course) right in the centre of the ulcer on the inside of his right leg. Dad described it as being 'like coring and apple'. A sizeable chunk of tissue was removed and sent off to histology, or wherever they take samples like that, to check for anything nasty. The results are expected in two weeks and I'll let you know Doll.

*****

I was crouching at your graveside, my mind muddled. While it still seemed impossible that you are gone, the harsh reality oozed into me again through the hand I placed on your stone. I mumbled my one-sided conversation to you, as so often I do.

'It's hard to imagine that this time two years ago you were just starting chemotherapy.'

I cast my mind back. You were so strong and I was crumbling under the strain.

'I miss you, Baby. I love you. Ciao, Mama!'

*****

I seem to be stuck with this stupid cough, although not all the time. It's always worse when I engage in conversation. Does that mean my vocal chords are involved? Perhaps.

In the bathroom mirror I've looked at the back of my throat and I can see that the tonsil scar on the right side of my mouth is white and raised (the other side isn't). I also see what looks like red and inflamed mucous membranes at the back of my throat.

I might yet make that doctors appointment.

I'll think about it at least.

*****

I had a chap round today to quote for painting the outside of the house. Pablo was recommended to me and although I haven't heard of the firm, it's local.

I have to get the woodwork and masonry painted, Darling, and it's just too much for me to tackle. And anyway, some of it is ladder work and you know I don't like heights.

He had a good look around and made notes. I counted seven windows, including the bay window at the front. Then there are the two garage doors and the door in the porch at the front, a back door on the garage and the new back door I have bought, but have yet to hang. On top of that, there are the fascias front and back and the rendering around the garage and the back of the house. You see? I can't do all that. I guess to a large extent it doesn't matter what it costs, I will have to pay someone.

Pablo said he will start in two months, which gives me time to sort out one or two things before any paint goes on.

*****

For most of this week we have enjoyed beautiful spring weather with plenty of sunshine and blue sky; a tonic for the body and mind.

Early on Sunday morning I visited Acorn Ridge in just such weather. The birds were singing and the whole place was bursting with bloom. Your plot was splashed with colour from cowslips and primulas, daffodils and forget-me-nots. The crocus leaves spelled out LOVE and your hawthorn tree seemed to be trying hard to survive.

After chatting with you, I went off around the site to view the names of others that you and I knew and some that I have become familiar with over the past eighteen months. It was sobering to see headstones that revealed the person's birth year to be the same as mine. I found a couple that morning. It was a slap that hit me hard.

1956.

And any birth year post '56, too. I don't suppose I had thought of it before, but it made me only too well aware of my own mortality.

My cough was almost gone and I didn't resort to the doctor, but you know of my little aches, pains and concerns.

1956.

Keep that tonic coming, Darling!

*****

Well, Linda, Dad's results have come back and they're saying he hasn't got cancer. That's really good news, but his legs are a mess, one worse than the other. Mum has been taking photographs of his ulcers for months, when the nurses have removed his dressings. And whilst there aren't many in the family who can bear to look, I have seen the images. I've also been there when the nurses have come, so I have seen his legs for myself. The nurses wash his legs, apply dressings and compression bandages, they make him comfortable. But the ulcers don't improve.

*****

Whenever I see a couple holding hands I feel robbed. Don't misunderstand me, Darling, I'm not angry with the couple for sharing their love in public, because that's exactly what we used to do. Nor do I feel pity for myself because I don't have you to hold my hand. I just feel robbed. We were always touching, cuddling, arm in arm.

I miss that.

I miss you.

*****

Notices have been put up at Acorn Ridge. They weren't around last week when I came. They're only small – about A5 size I suppose – but they carry a message that, in my view, is long overdue. They want visitors to follow the ethos of the site. Plastic must be removed from floral arrangements. No baskets, pots or containers and nothing to be hung from trees. The proprietors will remove anything which contravenes these rules (which are not new). Sorry, Darling, Abi's crystal may disappear, but I'm not going to be the one to take it out of the hawthorn tree. 'Watch the rainbows dance,' she had written in her note. When the sun shines and the crystal spins and sways it sprinkles rainbow dust all over you. It's beautiful.

We've been too long now without rain. I'm sure I heard on the radio this morning that we have had the driest March on record. We're now halfway through April and we still haven't had any decent rainfall. This does not bode well. We could either have a dry year, or else summer could get washed out!

*****

It's Monday and the start of another week. I've never understood why some people think a week starts on a Sunday, but they do. That's part of the weekend: the *week's end*. Your week, my week, always began on Monday.

So, Darling, after walking nineteen miles yesterday – practice for the Sarsen in a few weeks – I was, of course, very tired. I went to bed before 10.30 p.m. last night and went out like a light, but I woke in the small hours and went to the bathroom. Afterwards, I only managed another hour or so of sleep before the alarm went off. I struggled out of bed. The night had been one of unsettling dreams. I'm thankful that I can't remember them but I do know that I must have been in a lighter sleep to have had them at all.

I was out driving today and I played a CD by *'Flook'*. One particular track (*Wrong Foot Forward*) made me cry as I recalled the evening that you and I went to see them in The Forge at Basingstoke's Anvil. That was less than five years ago. Oh, how I miss you, Darling. As I've said to Wayne, my pain is only ever just beneath the surface. It feels as though getting on with life is merely distraction therapy.

But hey! I knew I had to snap out of my gloom. I hoped it was just that I was so tired.

*****

The weatherman reported on television this morning that yesterday was the hottest April day since 1949. Overall, he said, it is the hottest spring for a hundred years. Like the weather, my own life is parched since your passing. I do try to draw sustenance but I find only moisture when once I drank plenty. Every day I hope that I shall find a watering hole, lest I should wither up in the desert of my daily existence.

Although the warm and dry weather has been great, we are desperate for rainfall. Not that I want rain on my marathon walk next Sunday!

I'm on my last practice walk today, Easter Day. I've walked from Great Bedwyn, having got the train there this morning, and I am currently writing to you from the top of Ladle Hill, Burghclere, beneath what has been, virtually all day, a cloudless sky. It's a bit breezy and it's definitely cooler than yesterday, but still pleasantly warm.

As I look across to Beacon Hill I can see again the haze that has restricted my view for most of the day. It might be David Cameron's 'smog', of which he has been telling people recently. I can see the particles in the air. Well, not individually, but I can see the effect they are having. I find it interesting that the wind doesn't seem to be moving them on.

Now then, Blues, Dolly. Blues are the only ones I haven't seen. On the many recent walks I've done, the hills and woods have been teeming with butterflies. As well as little white feathers, butterflies make me feel that you are near. I know that, for many people, this makes no sense. How can you be, they might say, a fritillary on chalk downland one day and a Red Admiral in the garden the next? I don't see it like that. I can be on the hills in walking boots one day and lounging in the garden in flip-flops the next. What I feel, whenever I see a butterfly, is your presence. I even talk to you, such is the effect.

Most recently, I've seen Painted Ladies, Tortoiseshells, Peacocks, Wall Browns, Brimstones and Orange-Tips. There have been Vanessids, Browns, Yellows and Whites. But no Blues. Perhaps it's a bit early in the year.

Not too early for St. Mark's Fly, though! When I got up into Bedwyn Brail this morning the air was thick with them. You wouldn't believe it. Thousands or more swarmed before me as I battled against their buzz and their contact. They didn't bite me, but I used the folded map to bat them away as though they were a thick smoke interfering with my breathing. On and off, I've had them with me all day. Tomorrow is actually St. Mark's Day, so they have hatched out right on time.

I walked through the most beautiful bluebell woods today, carpeted with vividly coloured flowers that bring spring splendour and a smile to one's face. And the brightness of celandine and wood anemone only added to the joy of nature's gift. I know you would have loved it too.

After my stop at Ladle Hill, I made my way home by way of Burghclere and Greenham Common. I didn't realise how far I still had to go and this last section was hard on my body. Although I enjoyed my walk, I was exhausted when I got home and my entire body responded to my exertions. My feet were hot, although not blistered; my back ached and my neck felt tight; my hips were sore and my legs didn't seem to want to do what my brain asked of them. Sitting on an upright dining chair, I checked my map and was astonished to discover that I had walked 29 miles today. I forgave my body for complaining and hoped that it would be better in the morning.

*****

When I woke after a solid sleep, I had hardly any pain and was able to face the new day with renewed vigour. As daft as it might sound to other people, it warms me to think you had a hand in it and for that I am grateful.

I've written a poem Darling, inspired by my walking experiences.

The Noisy Pollinator

Hush!What noise as you flutter by me
on tiny, tinkling, paper wings
that whizz and whirr right past
and hue of brightest colour sings.
Listen! You tiptoe on every bloom,
guzzle and slurp light, fast,
then clap hard, flash pattern and zoom.
Hear! Colours sizzle in noon-day heat,
wings bang to make flight last
before you crash down lightly to eat.
Hark! The boom and bang of shapely din
explodes in a bright blast
of ear-splitting beauty, hearts to win.
Gush! How loud can a butterfly be?

*****

I just want to say, that right now, throwing anything away of yours is difficult. At best it is painful but at worst it's impossible. This morning I went to throw away your little red and white polka dot pumps that you bought for sister Linda's fiftieth birthday party, when the theme was the fifties. You'll remember that I Brylcreemed my hair into a DA and wore blue jeans and a tee; you tied your hair in a pony tail and wore a bolero cardigan, polka dot skirt, bobby socks and the red and white pumps.

I picked them up from the shoe rack today but I just couldn't throw them away. I don't want to see anyone else wearing them, so I've kept them. They take up hardly any room and I can, and do, occasionally pick them up to reminisce. The same goes for your sheepskin mules and the espadrilles you bought in a charity shop years ago. At the moment I can't bear to get rid of any of them. I think I am subconsciously, or perhaps consciously, associating your belongings with my memory and if I get rid of them I may be throwing away a bit of you – the memory of you – and I never want to forget.

*****

It's early morning and I'm walking The Sarsen Trail today. After my weeks of training, the day has arrived when I will set out to cover twenty six miles. The difference today is that there is money on it. Without giving anyone the hard sell I have clocked up £150 in sponsorship pledges, so I cannot fail now; must not; I dare not.

As I headed west along the A303, I was somewhere near Andover when I caught sight of the rising sun in my rear view mirror. It was getting on for six o'clock and the huge vermilion ball had just cleared the tree line behind me. Clouds, appearing to gather as if to discuss their options for the day, couldn't decide whether they should be light and wispy or dark and menacing. I scanned the morning sky. Red. That means *warning*, I thought, but if it would stay dry I could be happy with the weather.

I parked at Stonehenge and put on my walking socks and boots then locked the car and walked towards the coach pick-up. There was a strong wind that, as well as trying to blow everything away, lowered the temperature. I worried I wasn't prepared for this walk, that I'd worn the wrong clothing.

Every year, as you know, coaches transport participants from Stonehenge to Avebury and the journey by road takes around 45 minutes. The long walk back to the car starts at Avebury. I put on my wind-cheating waterproof jacket just before checking in. My start time was 7.15 a.m. There are always hundreds of walkers taking part in the event, but today, in their company, I walked alone.

At times, the wind was very strong and I had to lean into it to remain upright. When I reached the *19 miles to go* marker, I had been walking for exactly two hours. From experience, I knew that three and a half miles an hour was good, fast. In exactly three hours I arrived at the Redhorn vedette, a small building that the army uses as a guard post to cover live-fire exercises on Salisbury Plain. That was eleven miles into the walk. The remainder was all on the Plain, but there was no gunfire today. Just mile upon mile of gravel tracks edged with signs telling walkers not to stray as there could be unexploded ordnance. Incentive enough.

I passed the *7 miles to go* marker and hoped I had just two hours walking left, because I had now covered the distance that had lain before me after my first two hours of walking.

My total time for the course was 6 hours and 46 minutes. This was a personal record and I wished I could have shared my achievement with you. And, by the way, Darling, the weather wasn't too bad after all.

*****

Evenings are the worst, but it can be any time. I never know. My strange thoughts just come. I watch people and I wonder what they do in the evenings; what they do generally. What do I mean? I mean, for example, when they're driving where are they going? Home? A hotel? Holiday? Are they with someone? When they get there, will there be smiles and laughter, or will it all be sullen and serious? If they're walking, are they heading home after a long day at work? Will they settle down to something to eat and some rubbish television? Tell me Doll, am I the only person for whom this happens?

It's as though I have an urge to be a fly on the wall. I want to be on the outside looking in. Perhaps I want to be on the outside and look in at *you and me*, to watch our greeting; our kisses; to listen to that word *Love*, which we exchanged so often.

*****

I am not one of those people who say, simply, that we live and we die. When it comes to the matter of '*life after death*' I remain convinced that you saw where you were going. So tell me, my Darling, is there '*life*' where you are?

It's alright, I know, that's a daft question. And I can't hear your answer anyway, so please excuse my imagination.

Back here I conjure up fleeting images of you and everyone you are now connected with – family and friends, of course, and at one time, strangers – all getting on with one another at the best party ever. You had special invitations. No R.S.V.P was required because you were all definitely going, your Host made sure of that. Whoever and wherever He is, He's making sure you'll always be comfortable. None of His guests has the slightest pain; there are no furrowed brows; there is nothing for any of you to worry about. We do the worrying now instead. It's funny, looking back to the days following your departure, I remember those times when I thought you had only gone away for a while, thought that you'd be back from the party, or the holiday, or the visit. But I know you're there to stay. Reality has sunk in and I survive here because I know that one day my invitation will turn up and we'll be together. I'll be glad to throw off my aches and pains. I'll be very happy to check things out at the party, to look around and see who's there and then work out who's not.

This brings me on to talk a bit more about me and the Church: my religion; beliefs. I know I've always believed that someone really – I mean *really* – special was here all those years ago. I do struggle with the Old Testament, but some of the accounts in the New Testament fire my soul. What was it like back then? What was Jesus like? I try to place myself in his time and wonder about his birth, his early life and work, his effect on the people around him. I'm loaded with questions for which I will probably never have answers. How could he have been born of a virgin? Why did he lie low for so long before doing marvellous things that inspired people and got them thinking? How could he foretell his own death and then know he would be resurrected?

There is a passage in Hebrews that captures me. You and I even used it at St. John's when Father George blessed our marriage. In its most recent translation it reads '...faith is confidence in what we hope for and assurance about what we do not see...' Perhaps, then, I don't need the answers to the questions I've just listed. I merely need to have faith. Some of the things that happened to you and to us after your diagnosis made me wonder about faith. And what do we know anyway? If – as I think is the case – you saw and heard those who were at the party, then why is it so outrageous for us to imagine that Jesus did the same thing?

*****

After you died, I think I must have had a desire to strengthen my faith, but I had no plan in place. There has been no structure to the chain of events that have taken place and which continue in my life.

For example, Darling, the lent course leader has now asked me to have coffee with him in town. He wants to put me forward for confirmation in a few weeks and wants to talk some more about it. I'm still not sure, but he says the confirmation course I did with Wayne all those years ago, coupled with what we've been doing at Kip and Nina's, is a good foundation.

*****

Today is Sunday. It's another beautiful morning and the otherwise blue sky is dotted with fluffy, cumulus clouds that drift on a gentle breeze. Above them, in places, high stratospheric clouds appear to mark the edge of the sky like brush strokes on a wall. Between the clouds, vapour trails, some crisp and sharp, others loose and dying, scar the view from Acorn Ridge.

It's taken me an hour to walk here from St. John's church. I am trying hard to make the right decision as regards confirmation and I've come to ask if you can help me.

Should I even go through with it? Am I worthy enough? St. John's is willing me along, encouraging me. I want to feel closer to God, and yet I know I wrestle with some of the stories in the bible. Does this mean I'm not a true believer? I could not see all those things that you saw as your time grew short, but I believe in them. So perhaps after all I am beginning to form my choice simply by coming here and talking to you.

*****

'I would like to be confirmed because...'

I have to complete that sentence for my confirmation service. Yes, I have decided I am going to do it. I have a rehearsal on Tuesday then the actual service is next Sunday.

'I would like to be confirmed because I hope it may help me in my quest for a greater understanding of both life and death and bring me strength and inner peace as I prepare for my own journey beyond the divide.'

These are my genuine sentiments.

Thank you for your help, Dolly. x

*****

After mass this morning I talked to some of the ladies whom I have come to know over the months. Lynette had sponsored me for the Sarsen Trail, but I had not seen her since completing the walk.

'I kept you waiting, didn't I?' she made a softly spoken apology.

I had my photographs of the walk and handed them to Heather, who had also sponsored me and who had paid me the week after the walk. She asked if she could take the photographs home to view, so I promised Lynette that she could have them next week. Lynette, in her time, was an archaeologist with a special interest in Avebury and Stonehenge.

Sheila, seeing us gathered in the aisle, stopped to talk. She commented on Heather's new haircut, saying (as if Heather needed to be told) that it was a bit short. Although that was true, I didn't think it was for anyone to criticise.

'It'll grow back,' Heather said, trying to shorten her neck by raising her shoulders. 'Now I know how men feel when they have it all taken off!' She laughed off Sheila's comment.

Sheila told us that her son had once had hair half way down his back. She didn't mean it was growing on his back, but that it hung down that low.

'We had to ask him to get it cut,' she said. 'He was coming into the family business and we told him he couldn't meet clients looking like that. So he made the appointment. He walked up and down the street and passed the hairdressers three times before the hairdresser stepped out and said, 'For goodness sake, Chris, come in and do it.'

I chipped in: 'A bit like me with this confirmation thing. I've been walking up and down for months.'

*****

My confirmation service was quite beautiful. The Bishop of Reading, the Right Reverend Andrew Proud, was a warm and gentle man who conducted the proceedings with such serenity and eloquence that it was a joy to be confirmed. Mum came and so did Sarah, who I only phoned last week. I kept my promise and it was great to see her again. The support from these two ladies means a lot.

I knew for sure that I was doing the right thing.

I took the bread, but when the chalice was handed to me and I saw the contents, I was very emotional. After months and years of agonising and conscience, I was finally doing it.

When I sat back down after communion, I cried. And I think I did so because it is your death that had brought me to that point in my life.

*****

It's taken me a long time, Darling, and I mean a very long time, but today I finally replaced our back door. It's got three wooden panels at the bottom and six panes of glass above. I know you would approve.

Our friend Chris sourced the door from the merchants, then he and I measured the six panels and he arranged for a local glass company to make up double glazed units in toughened glass.

Alec had given me a hand last Tuesday with the first fit, but I couldn't leave the door in because there was no glass. After lots of messing about today, the glazed units are now in and the door has been hung. It's the door that both of us always wanted and I am pleased that I have managed to get it done before the painters start work. That won't be long now.

*****

This morning I went to the *Giant Car Boot Sale* at the racecourse. Of course, there weren't any giants and the cars weren't even that big, but I couldn't help overhearing a conversation as I walked round the stalls. It went something like this:

'Oh, hello, how are you?' There was surprise in the woman's voice.

'Hiya.' It was a jolly reply. 'I'm okay. You?'

'Yes, I'm fine thanks. Thought I'd take a look around. You never know.' There was a brief pause. 'Did you hear about Martin?' she asked the man she had met.

'Only briefly. What happened?'

'He came out of hospital and went back to work. Then he just dropped down dead.'

'Terrible,' the man said.

'Still, never mind,' the woman said.

Although I was merely ambling, I managed to amble away from any further conversation, but it struck me that the woman's description of poor Martin's situation was such that he had possibly had no impact on her life. I suppose I feel more sensitive because you are gone from us. And Brenda dying, David too, has affected me deeply. Death has touched me as never before, despite all those years I served in the emergency services. Even then, when I felt 'immune' to death, I am positive that I did not speak of anyone with the indifference I heard in the woman's voice. I am not suggesting that she was wrong, merely recording here another's attitude to death.

*****

I received another 'cold calling' letter today, this time from a well-known insurance company, its emblem brightening an otherwise plain white, windowed C5 envelope. In the window was your name, with that same typo already swapped among other companies. You're obviously on a database somewhere, Darling and, as far as all these irritating companies are concerned, you exist.

I thought I would go along with their assumption by returning the mail, unopened, to the address printed on the reverse of the envelope. I crossed through the window with a black pen and wrote beneath it,

> *'No longer residing at this address. Forwarding address unknown.'*

That's how it is now. You're always with me, inside my own head, but none of us has the forwarding address of those who leave us in the way you did.

*****

Blow me away with one of your little white feathers, they sent another letter exactly two weeks later. Perhaps they didn't believe what had been written on your earlier envelope. This time I decided to open it.

> *'Dear Mrs Page, you may recall that we wrote to you a couple of weeks ago with news of a special birthday offer on our Over 50s Life Insurance Plans.'*

I must have toughened up a bit, because a letter like this would have upset me not so long ago. There was more.

'This reassuring plan could give your family a helping hand when you're no longer around. It's designed to pay out a cash sum when you die...'

Now then, let me ponder their choice of words: *'when you're no longer around'*.

Is that what death means to this company? When you're no longer around, you are gone forever? Do they assume everyone thinks like that? What of the bereaved? Are they also to write off the deceased in the same way? Why didn't this company just use the word 'die' and remove what to me is a suggestion that nothing lies beyond the plane in which we live?

I know that for some of us, this is all there is. We live; we die. But if we're bold enough to use 'die' then at least we are left to imagine what might follow.

I was recently introduced to someone:

'This is Chris. He lost his partner two years ago.'

I immediately retorted.

'I didn't lose her,' I said. 'She died. My wife died. I know where she is.'

And whilst I may not know exactly where you are, it is certainly not the case for me that 'you're no longer around' because I feel you close to me every day. I talk to you.

Am I just being petulant? Should I lighten up?

Sorry, Dolly.

*****

Tonight, at Pat's invitation, I attended the first of seven evening sessions at St.Peter's in Bradfield Southend. The sessions form a course entitled, *'One Life. What's It All About?'*

I attended not because I've just been confirmed, but because I thought it would help me to make sense of the one life we all have. What is my life all about?

By the end of the session I realised that the one life is actually that of Jesus.

Silly me.

*****

Remember Darling, I told you last year Uncle Doug was not well, when Mum and Auntie Jean went out to Queensland? It was cancer; bladder cancer initially. I should have let you know at the time. Sorry.

Mum and Auntie Jean knew the situation and saw for themselves how tired their brother got. You know better than I how cancer can knock you flat and leave you more tired than you ever thought possible. Uncle Doug has been fighting the wretched disease and has had surgery, but it hasn't worked and the cancer has metastasised[4]. The only treatment for him now is palliative care.

Auntie Jean wants to go back again, to see him, but she would rather not travel alone and has asked sister Linda to go with her.

*****

I stood in the kitchen at breakfast time, waiting for the kettle to boil, and I saw my little note to myself on the counter top:

'Write to Wagamama.'

---

[4] Metastasis is the transfer of a disease from one part of the body to another by way of blood vessels, the body's lymph channels or across body cavities. In cancer, metastasis of a primary malignant growth results in secondary deposits, sometimes referred to as 'secondaries'.

It was my reminder that I wanted to write to the fast food restaurant to ask if they were okay with me using 'Wagamama' in the *Bright Lights and Fairy Dust* book. I stood there and thought the word over in my mind. It was you.

Then I thought back to your funeral, when I placed the Wagamama head scarf on your coffin with the single red rose. And because I was thinking about your funeral, I found myself rewinding further to your last few days with us here. And I wondered where you are now. And I remembered again the words you spoke that will stay with me until we are together again: 'I'm going, Chris.'

My Darling Linda, I am so empty and lonely without you that I'm sure when you died, a part of me died too. I am doing the best I can to keep busy, to prepare the house in case I decide to move, but this morning I am not doing well.

And I didn't write to the fast food restaurant, after all. Instead, I went on to their website and on the internet looking for the origins and meaning. It turns out, the Japanese translation of 'wagamama' is 'wilful little child'. Well, that's you to a tee. So I don't need to ask permission after all and I have one less thing to worry about.

*****

There's been a sudden change of plan, Dolly. I've been speaking with Linda and because she can't get the time off until the end of July, I'm taking her place and going to Australia with Auntie Jean. Uncle Doug is really unwell now and we think his time is short.

I'll apply for a visa and we'll go as soon as we can.

*****

You'd never know it was summer. After the long dry spell earlier in the year we just keep getting rain now. It has rained every day lately and I am feeling a little edgy about the painting of the house.

The painters were due to start last week, but the weather was so bad they put it back by a day. Claude and Vincent arrived on Tuesday but rain meant they could only work short days for the rest of the week. And the forecast remained 'unsettled'.

Pablo rang to tell me they weren't about to rush the job by slapping paint on in the sunny spells. No one could help the weather, he said, and, just as Claude had done on their first day, he assured me that they would not work in wet weather. Then he appeared to complain to me that all this rain had affected his work scheduling and was delaying other outside jobs he had. I felt as though I had transferred my stress and a load was lifted from my shoulders. Was that you doing that, Darling?

As challenging as it was for them and as stressful for me, they did get around to some of the painting. I was beginning to like the shade of green I had chosen for the doors and stone window cills, but by now I was also having serious doubts about the firm. I wasn't sure what to make of Claude and Vincent. They would always turn up early enough, but their work was frequently punctuated by cigarette and tea breaks. And Pablo only came to the house to deliver some ladders. I had expected him to be working on the job. He disappointed me in that regard.

*****

On Sunday I went to church under a cloudy sky. When I emerged from St. John's, all the cloud had been burned off and it had the makings of another Wagamama day.

I wanted to make the most of it and so when I got home, I loaded the car with all the cuttings from the pruning I had been doing in the garden beneath the gaze of Claude and Vincent last week.

I dropped the cuttings at the tip before driving to Acorn Ridge to tidy things up a little and to plant a bowlful of bulbs from your garden. I sneaked away a little more soil from the hump and smoothed off the rough edge that had developed. After planting your bulbs down either side of the hump I sprinkled the soil with grass seed. I hope you can help to make it grow.

By lunchtime the temperature gauge in the car was reading 30 degrees.

A complete change in the weather!

*****

Auntie Jean and I have got our visas and tickets for Australia and we're flying out the week after next. We've talked about how long we'll stay and agreed to go for three weeks, which I know is not a long time when one travels so far but I think that's about right for me. We're flying with Qantas.

I'll keep you updated.

*****

I've been fretting for weeks, ever since my fields test. I had missed a few lights with my right eye and was told I could expect to be called for a further appointment within a month. As you know, Darling, I now have annual checks for glaucoma because it's in the family. Pa was diagnosed years ago and I will never forget the tears he shed when he told me the doctors said he would go blind.

All morning I was restless, worried that I would hear bad news regarding my right eye. I saw the specialist at the hospital this afternoon. She dropped fluid into my eyes, which stung and made me cry, but it was necessary so she could check the pressure. She asked me if I had anything to report. I told her that I had been noticing that my right eye is not as good as the left, and also that the colours I see are different in that eye. It may be the beginning of a cataract, she said, but may not be anything to worry about right now. She checked my eyes thoroughly. Pressure was no higher than last year. The cups[5] are also unchanged. She had a really close look, with a light so small that unless it was aimed directly into the eye a person wouldn't even see it. But I saw it. And it was as bright as the sun and made me cry some more.

The specialist tried to allay my concerns by telling me that because I'm over fifty the changes I have

---

[5] The optic nerve is made up of millions of nerve fibres that bunch together and connect to the brain through the optic disc at the back of the eye (our 'blind spot'). The central portion of the optic disc is called the cup. This is normally quite small in comparison to the optic disc and measured as a 'cup-to-disc ratio' or 'CDR'. Damage to the nerve fibres, such as that caused by glaucoma, causes the cup to become larger. By monitoring the CDR, doctors can determine changes in the health of the eye and treat accordingly.

noticed are 'to be expected'. She is happy to see me in twelve months; no need for action today.

'Beautiful,' she said!

Although that's not an adjective I would have used, I was pleased with today's outcome.

*****

I was driving back from Winchester when I heard my mobile notifying me that I had a message. Then it repeated its warble, indicating another. The time was nearly 11.30 p.m. and I still had some way to go. I pressed on home and checked my mobile as soon as I pulled up outside the house. Wayne had sent me the same message twice:

> *Hey Pops,*
> *I've seen a post on Facebook.*
> *Are you awake? x*

I didn't want to do anything about his message at the time and, in any case, I had no credit left either to call or text him. If contact was to be made I would have to use the landline and it was too late in the evening for that.

When I stepped indoors and walked into the lounge, I saw that the landline answering machine was flashing. I couldn't bear to press the button that would retrieve the message.

As regards both telecoms, I had a feeling this would be the news that was inevitable. I didn't want to find this out on an answering machine, but would phone Mum and Dad in the morning.

*****

I left it as late as I dare, but I called them at 9.30 a.m. Clearly, something was amiss. Mum picked up the phone.

'Hiya, Ma. It's Chris,' I announced.

'Sorry you had to hear it on the answer machine,' she said.

'Mum, that's why I'm calling. I haven't listened to the machine. I figured something was wrong. I wanted to speak to you. What's happened?'

'Yes. Uncle Doug passed away last night.'

There was a short silence.

'He's at peace now,' she said.

This was indeed the news that we all dreaded and the core of Wayne's text.

Mum's fortitude at this difficult time was not lost on me. Her only brother, who is so far away, has died of cancer. I feel for Auntie Hilda and the family in Queensland; I feel for Mum and Auntie Jean here.

We're not flying out for another five days and it's sad that we won't see Uncle Doug. Whatever happens though, between us we will represent our families.

*****

Well Darling, I hope you approve of this paint job on the house, because I'm not sure I do anymore. I've been disappointed on every single day that the painters have turned up.

They came on recommendation, as I wrote earlier, but they don't seem to care much. There's paint on our garage floor now, because they have managed to spill it as well as stir it, and the step ladder they are using is missing rubber feet. As a result, the sharp metal edges have gouged into the roofing felt outside the bathroom window. I have tried hard to push my concerns to the back of my mind. I haven't raised them with the painters or with Pablo; I just want them to finish the job. I know I won't ask them back.

You and I knew the work had to be done. I can't do it because I can't do the high work. I also don't have the time. The bind is, it's taking much longer because of all the rain we've had.

Today, though, the painters worked late, making the most of the dry weather here in town.

*****

When it was clear to everyone that they weren't going to finish the job in the time they originally planned, Pablo turned up at the house to explain that he had other work coming up and would have to reschedule ours. It was at that point I decided to tell him about my forthcoming trip. But for the bloody rain he need never have known and the job would have been finished before I went. He also wanted payment for the work to date. Agreeing how far into the project they were was just one more thing that grated on me. Anyway, Love, I wrote him a cheque today and he has put me in his diary to start back in a month.

Australia

L ate on Monday evening, Auntie Jean and I left Terminal Three on a new-looking Airbus A380.

I watched our take-off using the Skycam, the live video feed to the seat-back screen in front of me.

By now we knew we wouldn't make it in time for Uncle Doug's funeral, which was unfortunate but understandable, as these things have to be organised in advance.

After booking our trip a couple of weeks earlier I had contacted our friends in the Blue Mountains and arranged to spend some time with them while I was in Australia. This would, I thought, take some of the intensity out of the situation in Queensland. My Aunties could have special time together without me in the background and I could catch up in person with Leonie and John in New South Wales. Leonie had asked over the phone if there was anything in particular I wanted to do and I suggested, despite my fear of heights, I'd like to climb the Harbour Bridge. She said she would organise things.

The Airbus was very comfortable Darling and I'm sure you would have loved it, but the flight to Singapore seemed endless. I made some notes in my journal that you might like to read.

At seven-thirty on Tuesday morning, UK time, two-thirty in the afternoon in Singapore, the IFE Flight Path screen advised that we were over the Bay of Bengal at 39,000 feet, travelling at 528mph, with 1,900 miles to go. We were still three and a half hours from Changi. A little while later, the screen updated anyone who wanted to view the information that our speed had increased to 570mph and it was minus 48 degrees outside. Not quite as cold as space, I guessed. Passengers and crew were instructed to fasten seat belts and almost immediately I felt the aeroplane lurching, rocking us like passengers in a bus on a dirt road. I navigated the screen back to the Skycam, Chopin nocturnes still playing in my earphones, and all I could see was rain lashing at the lens. I could only just make out the outline of the wings and the fuselage. I watched for several minutes before looking again at the Flight Path. We were flying over the Andaman Islands. We were still two and a half hours from Singapore. It was three-thirty in the afternoon there. The damned blinds were still down.
I was ready for something to eat and 'breakfast' was getting close!

We had a long wait at Changi Airport and swapped to a 747b for the next part of our trip. When the Captain advised us that the local time in Brisbane was nine minutes past midnight, I advanced my watch by two hours. It was now Wednesday.

Tuesday, the day of Uncle Doug's funeral, had been entirely wiped out by our journey.

At 8.30 in the morning I stood on the patio in Parker Street and looked out across the yard. It had been thirty one years since I was last there and much had changed, but there were aspects of the view that took my mind back all those years. And as I surveyed the scene I reflected on my Uncle's passing. I called to mind your passing; those terrible early days when my mind almost refused to accept what had happened. That part of grief that the experts call *denial*. Travelling to Australia though, brought it home to me that he really has gone from our lives.

I was tired. The patio seemed to move beneath my feet and I wobbled. After a whole day in the air, the notion that I was still flying was etched into my brain and I found myself compensating for it by placing my feet slightly apart.

All around me were the bright sounds of butcher birds, mynahs, kookaburras and magpies. I didn't know that they have come to know Auntie Hilda. They were telling her it was time she gave them breakfast. She put out meat for them but then also spread seed out across a tray for her regular vegetarian visitors. It wasn't long before the rainbow lorikeets lined up on the seed tray, treating us to a dazzling display of their colours.

Throughout the day, Auntie Jean and I were visited by our Australian relatives, some of whom I had never met.

By the afternoon the patio had slipped into shade and the cold of the Australian winter made its presence felt. I decided to walk round the block and step back into sunlight. It barely warmed me.

As I walked the ups and downs of this part of Goodna I saw for myself many homes that had been overrun by the horrendous floods that besieged Queensland in January. Through the front windows of unoccupied properties I could see how flimsy interior walls seemed to have dissolved, leaving skeletons of studwork. Although it was now several months on from the disaster, there was still a great deal of work to be done and many families were obviously still displaced. In some cases families had lost everything – *everything* – and I was shocked at the extent of the damage.

We had seen the news in the UK, but it was hard to appreciate the sheer scale of destruction. 'An area the size of France' is what I remembered being reported on all the news channels. How can anyone get their head around such a comment?

50 Parker Street was not entirely spared but, due to the topography of the area, whilst the floodwaters wrecked the yard, the house remained untouched.

*****

The following morning we drove to Richardson Park, next to the Goodna Rugby League pitch and clubhouse. These were high up on the lip of sandy cliffs that dropped away to the Brisbane River far below. Auntie Hilda explained that the river level during the floods continued to rise until it reached the top of the cliffs and spilled over into the properties around us. She said it had been suggested that water released from the Wivenhoe Dam was a major contributing factor in the Queensland floods at the time. I looked across to the countryside on the other side of the river and thought that probably everything except for the trees in the very far distance had been submerged.

At a Muffin Break in Redbank Plaza, the three of us enjoyed a coffee each before walking through the shopping areas. It was here that the thought came to me that I felt differently in Australia than I had in America. Somehow Darling – and I don't know how exactly – I was more relaxed about the place. Perhaps it was a bit more 'British'; the people a bit more like us back home.

There were many things, though, that ensured I was constantly reminded of just how far from home I was. Sunshine was the main one, of course. A big sky, azure and cloudless for two days in a row, was another. Shade cloths, stretched taut over steel frames above the Plaza car park, looked like ships' sails hung out to dry. It was winter and although the day was bright it wasn't particularly warm. But I had no doubt that on a hot summer day the shade cloths were essential.

*****

Auntie Jean and I had said 'Yes' when Auntie Hilda asked if we would like to see where Uncle Doug's service had taken place.

'*Heritage Park*' is a crematorium with memorial gardens. When we arrived I went straight up to the large glazed doors and pressed my camera against them in order to take a photo for Mum and Dad. I hadn't expected my flash to go off so when it did it came as no surprise that the man on the inside came up to the doors. I tried to wave apologetically, mildly embarrassed by the insensitivity I must have displayed, but the man opened the doors and asked if he could help me.

I explained that I was from England. I knew straight away that was a poor excuse. Auntie Hilda saved me from further embarrassment by saying the service for her husband had been carried out on Tuesday. We were invited in and I spent some time in deep thought and prayer for our dear Uncle Doug. Going to Australia had made me think hard about his death.

Before we left, the man at Heritage Park checked to see if Uncle Doug's ashes were ready for collection. He came back to the reception with an oblong box a bit bigger than a brick, which he presented to Auntie Hilda. It was a poignant moment and there was a brief silence all around. I felt for her bereavement, for Auntie Jean's and for my own. And, as sad and serious as I felt, I hugged Auntie Hilda outside the chapel and tried to offer some support. She was trying hard; her strength was amazing.

I don't want you to be annoyed Linda, that I spent just two nights at Parker Street before heading south. My time with my Aunties and my Australian family was precious. Now though, I was heading to the Blue Mountains; to more memories; to make new ones.

My flight was delayed more than once and I left Leonie a voicemail to explain that I was delayed due to 'a seafood spillage in the rear hold'. I will never know if that was code for something else, but it's what came over the tannoy.

Leonie was waiting for me at arrivals. As a result of the fish incident in Brissie, she had made the journey twice from her home. It took nearly two hours to get to Winmalee. My ears were uncomfortable and I had to swallow and yawn to equalise the pressure in them.

'Have we gained some height?' I asked.

'We've gained a lot of height,' she replied.

I felt it was cold in Sydney but it was even colder now in the Blue Mountains and when we got indoors I welcomed the warmth that came from the blown-air heating ('the air', as Leonie called it).

John wasn't well and hadn't been for five days. He had a chest infection now and after a little while he retired to bed and left Leonie and me to conversation over a glass of beer and a bottle of wine. It was inevitable that I would talk about my current situation, my feelings and my widowhood. We talked about you; your diagnosis; your treatment; your strength; your death. Leonie raised the matter of moving on. Of me moving on.

'You *will* love again,' she said. 'It's a fact that people who have been in a loving relationship don't remain alone. They need love, to love and be loved.'

*****

Leonie and I went for a walk down the road. It was unfortunate for John that his chest infection kept him in bed and he wasn't up to coming with us. *Down the road* was nearly an hour's drive away. Leonie took me to The Valley of the Waters and Wentworth Falls in the mountains. We were going bush walking. She had a thing about water and waterfalls. There was something magical and enchanting about them.

After parking the car we began our trail. There were some steep steps leading down to an observation platform, from where I looked out across the beautiful Blue Mountains. I could hear the sound of running water far below us, the source of which was hidden from view by a dense canopy of trees.

'Is there a river down there?' I asked, as though I had just made an important discovery. It was a daft question. After all, we had gone to see waterfalls.

As we descended more steps Leonie issued a friendly warning.

'Remember, Chris, for every step you go down there's one to go up again.'

At the time it only struck me as an obvious fact. I wasn't concerned at all. On the way down, the steps got steeper and there were handrails to assist walkers and keep us from falling over sheer drops. The walk became something of a challenge and then Leonie's warning made sense. She's been here before, I thought.

At Empress Falls, the source of my earlier query, we stood for a while; listened to the cascade; watched it tumble over the rocks and drop into the gorge below. On our way further down we passed warning signs advising walkers that due to landslides creek crossings could be difficult and paths awkward to negotiate. Undeterred, we pressed on and soon appreciated what the signs had meant. It became a physical challenge for both of us, at times requiring a hand from one or the other to scramble up a rock or ease a steep jump. Way down in the gorge it was cool and shaded. Through gaps in the canopy I saw that the sky was blue and cloudless. Every now and then I caught glimpses of sun-kissed rock faces, golden in colour and revealing the strata of millions of years of sedimentation.

When we came to one of the many forks in the path, we chose to head for the highlight of our bush walk today. The visitor sign read 'Wentworth Falls via Slack Stairs' and we began to climb out of the gorge. The path, often only a foot wide in places, twisted and turned this way and that. We clambered over fallen trees and loose rocks, made hairpin turns on sheer rock faces, caught sight of the Wentworth Falls, all the while only climbing slowly. It was not a walk that could be rushed.

Then we came to Slack Stairs, a series of metal stairs affording us a way up steep-sided rocks that would otherwise have terminated our walk right there. The steepest of the stairs was more like a ladder and it was enclosed in a metal safety hoop. You know me and heights, Darling!

'Good practice for the bridge climb,' I suggested.

We crossed stone clapper bridges over flat pools half way to Wentworth Falls and came to the 'Grand Staircase'. It was appropriately named. Looking up at our way ahead we saw a golden staircase, hand carved from the sandstone edge, with steel cables bolted to the cliff face and a high handrail on the outside to keep us safe from the sheer drop. The climb was hard, but our destination was spectacular.

And for every step we had gone down...

Back at Conservation Hut – our starting point – I read the visitor information board.

> *Bush walkers should always take sufficient supplies of food and water, give details of their route to a responsible person and pick up a PLB*

location beacon free of charge from the NSW police or State Emergency Service.

We had done none of this.

Leonie chuckled. 'It was a tourist trail, Chris. It's when people go off the path and into the bush that they get into trouble.'

*****

I went for a walk to the Winmalee shopping centre, about a mile and a half from John and Leonie's home. This was a completely different experience for me from my stroll in New Jersey. I passed many other walkers and even saw cyclists. Most of them exchanged a greeting with me.

*****

We were on our way to the city, Leonie driving. She passed me the iPad just minutes before we ran out of morning.

'Here, Chris, you can be the navigator. I'm not sure how to get to Cumberland Street.'

I lifted the leather cover.

'What do I do? I've never used one of these before.'

'Just clear that box in the top right, then type in *Bridge Climb*.'

We walked across George Street to Circular Quay. Ferries, hydrofoils and catamarans pollinated the city as passengers stepped out into Sydney. The Opera House, its voluminous curves blending with cool, pale clouds, stood sentinel across Sydney Cove. The Overseas Passenger Terminal, where leviathans of ocean transport would tie up, although empty that day, afforded us a tantalising glimpse of our forthcoming adventure. The grey steel framework of the Harbour Bridge stood out against the sky like a giant Meccano kit and there, just below the Australian flag at the very top, we saw a string of bridge climbers. As tiny specks on the superstructure, they highlighted its sheer size.

'We should get going, Chris. Can you remember the directions?'

I glanced at my watch.

'I think it's two blocks over. We're okay for time. Let's go up through there.'

We zig-zagged through some of the oldest streets in the country and arrived at the entrance to Bridge Climb with the required fifteen minutes in hand.

After introductions to our fellow climbers and our climb leader, Mitch, we were kitted out. It seemed that Sydney had saved its coldest day for twenty years just for me. The wind chill out on the bridge, we were told, was six degrees, so we were provided with extra clothing in addition to the rear-zip boiler suit. Windproof overpants, a fleece in a bag and gloves were issued. Every item of clothing had to be clipped on to D-rings on our boiler suits. We weren't permitted to take anything of our own out on to the bridge. Even handkerchiefs were supplied, attached to wrist bands.

Mitch was young, enthusiastic and loaded with quips and funny stories almost certainly intended to put us at ease and encourage us. He equipped us with radio packs and headphones and began his commentary.

'This way folks.' He paused. 'Chris, you're my back marker. You okay with that?'

I had no way of knowing.

'Fine,' I said, smiling.

The cowstail from our waist harness was clipped to the safety line and the experience began. A short tunnel cut through rock and concrete led to a narrow catwalk.

I could not walk out along the catwalk as quickly as Mitch and the others. Even stepping out from the tunnel was a leap of faith. I had to trust that the two planks beneath my feet would not come loose or snap and that, even if they did, my harness and running line would stop me from falling to my death. The distance between me and Leonie (she was the climber in front of me) stretched out and my heart pounded with fear. With Mitch's commentary in my headphones I tried to focus on a view other than a downwards one.

When we reached the first pylon, one of the four structures that appear to hold the bridge together, I felt I had a bit more than nothing beneath my feet. We were told that the pylons don't actually contribute to the strength of the bridge but were built to give that impression. In the 20s and 30s, when the bridge was built (it was completed in 1932) all-steel bridges were a new concept and many people didn't trust them.

We climbed a series of steel staircases within the pylon, up to a gantry. Mitch explained that we now had something called a 'squeeze through' to negotiate and we went up through the deck of the bridge to the topmost curve; the curve of the 'coat hanger'. By this time I had caught up to the rest of the group, but only because Mitch had bunched us as we began the long climb to the top. Half way up, we stopped for a photo. Mitch had the only camera. Although he kept it in a case, the body of the camera was connected to a D-ring. If he lost his grip, it wouldn't end up puncturing a motorist's car roof or sinking to the bottom of the Paramatta River.

On the outside of the steelwork I felt comfortable now. I had faced my fears. When we reached the highest point we were taken across another gantry, which crossed between the two flags and beneath the flashing red navigation light. One by one, each climber stopped directly under the light to make a wish. If we looked up and the light was on, our wish would come true. My red light was a split second out. A shame, because I could have made good use of what I'd wished for.

Mitch held us at the top, waiting for the afternoon light to fade. As it did so, the city gradually replaced it with a glow of its own. We gazed down at Luna Park on one side and Circular Quay and the city high-rise on the other. Connecting the light shows was the red and white necklace of traffic crossing the bridge on the Bradfield Highway far below us.

He took the last photos of the day and we began our descent, down ladders through the train deck then along the catwalks from the pylon to a second tunnel cut through the bridge stanchion.

Leonie and I compared our steel adventure to our bush walk four days earlier and we both agreed that there were similarities. The climbs, gradients and squeeze throughs and the time we had spent on the bridge were all proportional to what we had experienced in The Valley of the Waters. And we had appreciated both. She spoke to Mitch.

'Chris didn't tell you he was scared of heights.'

'You didn't look it. Out there on the bridge you were so relaxed.' Mitch smiled at me. 'I'm glad you were my back marker Chris.'

'Thank you, Mitch,' I said, 'that was awesome.'

*****

On my last night in New South Wales John, Leonie and I sat down to a curry. I was pleased for John that he was finally coming through his illness.

Now, you know, Linda, I could eat curry every day, and this one was very good. I thanked my hosts for their kindness and hospitality and, although it didn't need to be explained, told them that I had only been able to afford to come to Australia because of what had happened to you. It was always on our list as something we wanted to do together.

The three of us raised our glasses and drank a toast.

'To Linda!'

I felt my tears welling as I thought of you. My pleasure, throughout my time so far in Australia, was always tempered with the sadness of your passing and that of Uncle Doug.

I gave John and Leonie a little poem I had written:

Dear John and Leonie

As I pass now from the embrace
Of your warmth and kindness
Once more will we be far apart.
Yet may I not soon see your face
Our friendship is timeless
And forever close in my heart.

With love to you both
Chris

*****

Leonie was booked on a course in the city. In the run up to my visit to New South Wales she and I had exchanged emails and my stay had been arranged to fit in with her course. She would drop me off at the airport on the way into Sydney.

'I've got butterflies,' I said, as we approached the domestic terminal.

'Why?'

'I'm worried I won't have time to get through security and I'll miss the plane.'

Leonie laughed. As she pulled up at the drop-off zone she tapped the car clock.

'See? You've got plenty of time.'

It was 8.10 a.m.

We said our goodbyes in the car. I was sad to be leaving but, of course, I had to go.

'Thank you, Leonie, for everything. You're amazing. You're busy all the time. I don't know how you do it.'

'It was a pleasure, Chris. You fitted right in with the house. Keep in touch. And keep in touch about your love life.'

We hugged across the cabin.

'Don't get out,' I said. I jumped out and reached in to the rear seat for my backpack. 'Thanks again for everything.'

As I walked away I turned back and blew Leonie a kiss, which she returned, adding a wave and a broad and pretty smile.

My two Aunties were waiting for me at the Brisbane Domestic Terminal. Again, I had the feeling that these internal flights are just like using the bus or train, only quicker. Sorry, Darling, if that sounds obvious, but this was all a new experience for me.

It took about an hour to get back to Goodna. I put my backpack in the lounge at Parker Street, shed one jacket, then another before sitting out in the yard with Auntie Hilda and Auntie Jean. The sky was big and blue, and that part of the patio that was in the sun was cosy and warm. It was only a few degrees warmer than Sydney, but they made a difference.

I realised that sadness had washed over me again. I was back at Uncle Doug's home, but he wasn't there. In my head I suppose I was looking for him. He has left his mark everywhere: in the landscape he and Auntie Hilda have created with their planting, beneath the pergola where we were sitting, in the things he has collected over the years.

As the conversation flowed, I couldn't help feeling that he would walk in and dispel the reality of our bereavement.

*****

We drove into Ipswich. I could not remember coming to the town in 1980 and considered this my first visit. I spotted a church and wondered if we might be able to get inside, so we walked up to the doors of St. Paul's Anglican Church and to my delight were permitted to enter. Built in the Revival Gothic style of plain brick with stone mullioned stained glass windows, it is the oldest Anglican Church in Queensland, construction having started in 1855.

The craftsmanship of the builders and carpenters was a joy to behold. The stained glass was crisp and bright and the light entering the church through it was warm and golden. I approached the altar and bowed my head then took a seat on one of the front pews.

I had a quiet word.

*****

Brisbane was established as a penal colony in 1825. It was opened up to free settlers in 1838 and given city status in 1901.

When my Aunties and I emerged from Central Station I saw how much this 'big country town', as locals once referred to it, had grown. Tall high-rise buildings, perhaps deserving in some cases of the title 'skyscrapers', reached for the sun and in so doing held entire streets in shadow.

I was pleased to see that many of the old facades have been retained and there are still places that reflect Brisbane's early days. Buildings of sculpted sandstone, if the sun was permitted to land on them, returned a rich, warm glow and a myriad shadows from relief mouldings or cornices. At first sight the old and the new, I thought, came across as something of a shock, but ultimately fitted well together. Like a modern library containing the latest books, the old first editions were still important and not at all out of place.

*****

I can't remember how it came about, but today I took charge of the oblong box that had come from Heritage Park. We were taking some of Uncle Doug's ashes to scatter on the football pitch where he had played and coached.

It was the last full day of our stay in Australia and the family assembled at Kippen Park, Goodna, home of the Western Spirit Football Club.

In memory of Uncle Doug the club named the pitch on which we now stood *The Doug New Field*. As a player, he had been a winger and so those who wanted to took some of his ashes and scattered them on the touchline on either side of the pitch. I thought it was a fitting tribute.

During our short time in Queensland Auntie Jean and I met all our relatives who live there. The children I saw thirty years ago have children of their own now and, of course, the family has grown.

The time had come though, to say goodbye to most of them as we prepared for our return to the UK. Our Australian family may be 12,000 miles from where we live, but they are always close in our hearts.

*****

Saying goodbye to Auntie Hilda at the airport was difficult for all three of us, but we will meet again soon enough, when she visits the UK. There are things that she must do both in Australia and in the UK that will take a little time to work through.

Auntie Jean and I flew to Singapore on a Qantas 747. I was looking forward to getting back on the A380 when we got there. Alas, it wasn't to be. The Airbus was delayed and we were put on a British Airways 747 instead. We had a long and tiring flight home but everyone knows that's what one endures after visiting the other side of the world.

*****

Once home, I looked forward to seeing the house painting finished. With just over a week to go before

Claude and Vincent return, I thought I would help things along by undercoating the front and back doors for them. You can probably sense my impatience, Darling, but I am desperate to have the job completed so that I can wave goodbye to the painters.

*****

Auntie Amma wasn't my real auntie, but that's what we all called her when we were growing up, until we grew tall enough that we could drop the 'Auntie' and still remain respectful. And her real name wasn't Amma either. It was Alma. We just never could pronounce the 'L'.

Alma featured a great deal in our lives. She and her husband, Josif, lived next door to Mum and Dad. They only moved out this year and only then because they had become old and dependent. Josif is in his nineties, deaf and almost blind. Alma, who was never one to venture far, had suffered from agoraphobia and depression. We didn't know that as kids. She was there for us; I mean, right *there.*

As a child I was aware, I remember, that their last name was unusual and difficult to spell. Although Auntie Amma was from our town, Josif was Yugoslavian and it was only when I was older that I understood all this.

Josif never learned English well, but whether that was by accident or design I do not know. He would grunt words and string them together sometimes without verbs, sometimes without prepositions. His facial expression would help me to understand him. A smile, broad and white against his dark skin, was a sign that he was trying to say something nice. It might be that he had some potatoes or runner beans for Mum and

Dad from his precious vegetable garden – his pride and joy. A frown and his words might be intended to dissuade troublesome children from stepping on his hard work.

We often heard Auntie Amma shouting, mostly at Josif, but he always seemed to ride out her tirades with ease, or else walk off to the pub for his regular tipple. She would have calmed down by the time he got home.

As they got older and while I still lived at home, to me they were ageless. I never noticed the changes. But most recently I could see they were both in decline. Alma was diabetic and wore thick-lens spectacles. She was frail and old; eighty one now. Josif was ten years her senior. Despite his situation, he regularly made his way to that same pub and back. More recently, friends would pick him up or drop him home.

The deterioration in their health, and the care that was necessary to look after them, were the reasons they had moved out this year into warden assisted accommodation. The housing estate had lost two more old-timers.

Last week, Alma was admitted to hospital because her blood sugar levels were unstable. Initially, she was making good progress, but she suffered a massive heart attack and died later in the hospital.

Today I went to Auntie Amma's funeral.

As many of our family as could make it turned out to wave her farewell. It was a small affair because Alma was denied the privilege of close friends. But for me it was a privilege to have attended her service.

*****

The painters came back today and in good weather too. However, since they were last here Vincent's thrown the towel in and Pablo has sent Leonardo in his place. The latter's only job was to top coat the doors.

Give me strength, Darling! I didn't think I was that brilliant at painting but oh dear, please let this torture end.

*****

As I have told you many times before, it is rare for me to dream about you. I have so often wished that you would come to me in my sleep, but it has only happened a few times. Last night though, you fulfilled my wishes.

> *I was sitting down in an area that appeared to be the inside of a village hall. I had my back to the wall. You came along and stopped briefly and looked down at me. You smiled. You were beautiful. I saw your almond eyes, dark skin and dark hair. The images were so vivid I thought them to be real. Two other people were with you. One of them was, if I can use this description, 'small', although that might mean 'young' or 'younger'. I could not make out whether the two people were male or female. I don't think I recognised them.*
>
> *I held out my hand. You reached out and took it in yours.*
>
> *I said, 'Oh, Baby, I miss you. Why have you come? I know you will go away again.'*
>
> *I began to cry. As you squeezed my hand, as if to reassure me, I woke up.*

I was distressed.
Had you come for me?
Are you getting ready to do so?

*****

I haven't slept well since you died. There may have been a few nights when I seem to have gone right through, but they are rare. I usually wake these days even before six.

And so it was this morning. In fact it was five o'clock, but I hadn't woken up without a prompt.

In my sleep, or in my dream, no visuals to recollect, I heard someone's voice. A single word was uttered, once to rouse me and then once more:

'Chris.'

*****

I had a funny turn today, which is not something I'm used to. Luckily for me I was in bed when it happened, but it was still very frightening.

I had spent the morning at home. I was fine, apart from having the awful taste of Corsodyl in my mouth, which I had swigged earlier to help combat some oral discomfort.

At lunchtime I made and ate a round of cheese sandwiches and followed that with some fruit yoghurt. All was well. I should mention, Darling, that I had woken up with a sort of 'clamping' headache that gave me spasms of discomfort. It was the kind of headache I've had when I have been dehydrated. Anyway, I made sure I drank plenty of tea and coffee this morning.

After eating, I went upstairs to the study to continue working on *Bright Lights*. I wasn't at the computer long when I felt incredibly tired. I couldn't concentrate; just wanted to sleep. I took myself on up to the crow's nest and set the alarm clock for one hour. It was, by now, just after two o'clock. I kicked off my slippers and didn't feel I needed to get undressed as I was only going to power down for an hour. I eased myself into the bed, pulled the quilt over me and turned on to my side.

About ten minutes later – and I know this because I raised an eye to the clock when it happened – I was disturbed by pounding within my chest from a heart that felt like jelly. I felt giddy. My breathing increased spontaneously and I added to this by making a point of filling my lungs with as much air as I could take in.

Strange thoughts came to me:

- That I might die.
- That I *had* died.
- That I was unable to raise the alarm. I could be there ages before anyone found me.
- What would people say?
- Who would finish your book?
- It is not time yet.

Once again, as I write this note to you, I wonder if I am being prepared.

*****

Today, I went to another funeral.

As was the case with Auntie Amma, Raoul Poulain had always been in our lives. There aren't many people about whom I can say, 'I have always known him or her,' but Raoul was one of them. A lovely man, and popular, he and his wife, Sylvie, were the neighbours opposite Mum and Dad. They had three children: Dion, Gilles and Juliette.

Raoul's funeral was, not surprisingly in consideration of his life, well-attended. It was a *good* church service, if that is an appropriate way to describe any funeral (I know people have described funeral services as *lovely* too) but, as ever, it set off a range of emotions in me that made me reflect on my own situation.

Gilles read a poem in the church:

Miss Me

When I come to the end of the road
And the sun has set for me
I want no rites in a gloom filled room.
Why cry for a soul set free?

Miss me a little, but not for long
And not with your head bowed low.
Remember the love that once we shared,
Miss me, but let me go.

For this is a journey we all must take
And each must go alone.
It's all part of the master plan,
A step on the road to home.

When you are lonely and sick at heart
Go to the friends we know.
Laugh at all the things we used to do.
Miss me, but let me go.

I had no idea, Linda, until I looked it up on the internet, that this is another of Christina Rossetti's poems. Even as Gilles stood up in church I thought, 'oh dear, here we go with another funeral poem that's supposed to give us something to cling to'. I think, to start with, I didn't give it my full attention until the end of the first verse. And then I thought that it did make sense and, in particular, the line *'a step on the road to home'*.

* * * * *

I haven't seen our granddaughters for two months and I am excited at the prospect of seeing major changes in them. Wayne says Darcy has started to crawl and Lola is standing. The girls babble on at one another in a language of their own. Darcy has almost all her teeth.

I was travelling by train to Paddington. Wayne has arranged to collect me from there.

The journey was extremely uncomfortable on my ears. I don't know why, but I get upset at certain frequencies and by pressure. It brought back a particular memory; a painful memory:

> It was a bright summer's day and we had attended a wedding reception at Greenham. We had to break off to drive home to feed Burma and let him out for a pee. It was a hot day. You wanted the window down in the car. I couldn't stand it, the buffeting, painful in my head. I put the window back up. You put it down again. I was desperate. I flicked your hand away from the button on the centre console and put the window up again. You wrestled my hand away. I lost my

self control and flipped out. I nearly did the same to the car. You cried all the way home, but you let me keep the window closed. I was horrible I know and I am forever sorry. But it hurt me, Dolly. Hurt my ears.

And the memory still hurts and haunts me.

Today I was half way down one of the three carriages. Several of the top windows had dropped open during the journey. My head was being buffeted by the violent inflow of air and there was nothing I could do about it.

*****

I thought – and it turns out I was mistaken – that today was the tenth anniversary of 9/11, the terrible attack on America.

I recalled what I saw on television that awful day and I pray for everyone who died, for all those who were bereaved, for the many, many people who worked to rescue trapped and injured victims.

I also pray that such a thing will never happen again, but I fear that it will.

And I spare a thought for everyone who, like me, has been affected in some way.

But the main reason I am writing to you today is because I had another disturbed night. There is no pattern to them. I have tried going to bed early and late, have cut out the caffeine drinks in the evening, even cut out the alcohol. I never know how my sleep will go.

This morning I woke at 5.24. There didn't seem to be a reason. I didn't need the toilet; wasn't cold (or hot). I suppose I then drifted into very light sleep, because I had a bit of a dream, one I would like to share:

I was sitting in the armchair at Mum and Dad's house. On the carpet in front of me was a beige-coloured eye shade, like the ones you get on an aeroplane on a long haul flight. Mum and Dad were both in the room, Mum behind me I think. We were all very relaxed. Then Dad got up and came over to where I was sitting. He was younger than his years in my dream and he had no ailments that I could discern. He leaned down to me, kissed me then cuddled me, cheek to cheek.

'I love you, Son,' he said. 'I'm going on up now.'

I woke up and pondered the significance of my reverie.

*****

I played in the band tonight.

We were half way through a ceilidh, a double 50th birthday celebration, and were on a break for food and refreshments. I tried to make up my five-a-day from the gourmet buffet, which was very tasty. We were the first to get food and were seated at a table that had been set up in the middle of what would become the dancing area. Directly in front of us was a screen that seemed to be linked to an overhead projector, which in turn appeared to be connected to a laptop. The machine worked through loads of photographs of the birthday couple and as the images appeared on the screen an iPod blasted out seventies and eighties music. Perhaps the iPod wasn't linked after all, but it was loud, and right in front of us.

The couple were clearly well-travelled, judging by the photographs that were selected. The pictures also revealed much about them both: university educated; children; sporty; active. Oh, Linda, I found myself feeling sad that we have been parted. You and I were going to retire together and spend time together.

I knew it was wrong to feel envious of another's good fortune; wrong to compare my situation to theirs. So I stepped away from the party for a moment to write these notes to you. I was in a back room, behind the stage, on my own. It is as easy to feel alone in a packed hall.

The iPod continued to push out loud music and I couldn't help thinking this couple should have had a disco rather than a ceilidh. Mind you, it might have been difficult to dance to some of the music I heard.

I hoped the second half would go well for us and for the guests.

'Come on!' I admonished myself.

It was nearly nine o'clock. We had two hours left to play. I knew I had to get on instead of feeling sad and lonely.

Sorry, Dolly.

*****

When I woke this morning I wasn't even sure what day of the week it was until the radio alarm kicked in. Then I realised that *today* is actually the tenth anniversary of 9/11. I don't know what I was thinking when I wrote it last week!

Anyway, I got up and dressed myself all smart for church. Mass was at eight. In his sermon, Father Trevor made much mention of the need to forgive – in spite of the terrible events all those years ago.

Can we?
Will we?

*****

I was working in our garden this afternoon when I realised that your birch tree – the one you planted at the bottom of the garden – had shed some pale yellow, heart-shaped leaves. Looking up from the carpet of dead foliage, I saw that the entire tree had turned colour and it was, of course, because leaf fall has begun. Autumn has officially arrived. Nature is truly amazing. Only two days into it and already one of our trees knows what it has to do.

The tilt of the earth at this time of year means that we are leaning away from the sun, which remains low in the sky. The days are shortening, the light has changed. Nature knows that and so do you.

Soon our garden will be covered in fallen leaves and autumn colour. I shall be required to collect them and stuff them into our green bin. The Local Authority will arrange to have the contents taken away and – along with everyone else's garden refuse – turn them into a soil conditioner.

Next year, we can put it down to help spring growth.

*****

It's been a long time, Darling. Do you know how much I've wanted that belly bar back?

I went back to the tattoo parlour today. I'm pleased and will make sure I look after it better this time.

*****

I walked to Acorn Ridge. I stopped twice. Once to draw cash from the ATM and once to write down some verse that came into my head. It's not very good, but here it is anyway:

> *Be not afraid to call my name*
> *Whether in joy or in sorrow.*
> *I will still love you, just the same.*
> *I have left you this verse for tomorrow*
> *When we shall begin the life*
> *in which we touch*
> *not with our bodies,*
> *But with one heart and mind.*

I was trying to write as though the words had come from the other side after one's death. It hasn't really worked has it? I know. Sorry.

Oh, well, back to my walk. Even with those breaks, I still got to Acorn Ridge in 1 hour 20 minutes. The weather started out dull and grey but when I got there the sun was shining in between what I'll call 'Constable' clouds, warming up the hillside nicely. A breeze rustled the weakening autumn leaves and wafted the scent of new-mown grass across my face.

It was with genuine surprise that I saw a hearse in the car park. At first, because there were lots of cars there, I just thought Acorn Ridge was particularly busy. Then I realised that I had arrived at the same time a funeral was taking place. I wanted to give them room; wanted to show some respect. I felt a tiny bit awkward, but then thought I had as much right to be there. I passed a few mourners who were gathered in the car park then I walked down the right hand hedgerow.

I perched on a bench that was engraved with the words, '*Loved always*' and took out my notebook. I let the sunshine light my pages and my face and thought to wait a while for the funeral party to disperse.

Oh, Gosh! 'Funeral party'. When I think these words, or say them, for a moment they don't seem to go together. I know that in this context 'party' doesn't mean fun and celebration.

But the moment fades.

After fifteen minutes I sat with you at last, comfortable that I afforded the mourners space and time enough.

Wayne is coming on Tuesday. We are only days away from the second year of your passing. I wanted to know that everything at Acorn Ridge was tidy and as neat as I could make it. It is almost unbelievable that so much time has passed.

*****

In the summer – I don't know exactly when because it was a process rather than a single event – I took away some of the photographs I had of you around the house. It wasn't an easy thing for me to do, but I had begun to think the house might have been on the way to becoming a sort of shrine to your memory. There were more photos than I realised and there was something of you in almost every room. I hope you can forgive me, Darling. I didn't take them all away, but I have read and heard of people who have done the 'shrine' thing. Although on the one hand I can't help thinking it's a little strange, on the other I don't think ill of those who choose to do it. In my current situation, I can see how they might lean that way. But if *I* can think it strange, then other people might think the same of me and I don't want family and friends to feel awkward when they visit.

*****

I have a wrinkle on the left side of my face. I didn't take too much notice of it at first, but the damned thing is so creased now that I will never be rid of it. When I sleep on my left side at night, I dare say I am only ensuring the permanency of the fold in my skin. Only the other day, not long after I had shaved, I had a bit of an itch on my face. It turned out it was a little bit of moisture trapped in my wrinkle.

I conclude that I am a wrinkly.

*****

Wayne and Sara brought Lola and Darcy to the East Fields this morning. We had organised a little tea party to celebrate their forthcoming first birthday.

The little ladies were at first overwhelmed by their new surroundings and by all the people who came to wish them happy birthday. However, when lunch was on the table and they were seated in their high chairs, they were happy enough to get on with feeding and playing. As much food landed on the floor as made it into their tummies, but it was great to see them enjoying themselves.

*****

Can I write *11111* as a date?

No, I thought not. But our granddaughters were born on a date that was a palindrome. I just wanted to echo the fun of that on this, their first birthday.

Wayne and Sara were back in London with them now. I sent an early text at quarter past seven:

> *A happy, happy first birthday to you, Lola, and to you, Darcy, with love from your Grandpa Pops.*
> *Have a zootastic day with your folks! xx*
> *Love to Wayne and Sara.*
> *Thinking of you all.*
> *xx*

Wow! A whole year! Wayne had told me previously their plans for the day.

I received a text straight back:

> *Thanks, Grandpa Pops. It's looking dull up here, so we're gonna hit The Aquarium.*
> *We love you.*
> *xxxx*

Okay, so the zoo was off now, but nonetheless I guessed the ladies were already preparing for their special day. In my mind's eye I could picture The Aquarium on the South Bank. You and I had walked past it when we had that special day in town that our babies organised. I remembered the grandeur of the building and how it impressed me with its Portland Stone frontage, its pillars and windows, indeed its very shape. We probably could have visited The Aquarium, but chose the Imperial War Museum instead.

It didn't stop me now from recalling the location and our time together.

*****

I went to the Bereavement Support Group coffee morning in Calcot: our monthly gathering and a chance to catch up with one another and – more importantly – to support one another. I took Dennis again. It's great that we can all share a laugh or two in company. Any opportunity to lighten our day is most welcome.

When I got home I checked my e-mails. The publishers had sent me the fourth proof of *Bright Lights and Fairy Dust*. I printed and checked it thoroughly, which took me all evening. I didn't read every single word because I was only checking for typesetting and layout issues. The content had already been signed off.

*****

I was happy that I was able to approve this version and I sent it back to the publishers this morning. Now I must wait for them to send me the cover for the book for approval.

Mum called in for a cup of tea on her way to the supermarket. As we sat and talked, I passed on the good news that I had finally approved the *Bright Lights* proof.

The subject of Christmas came up and I said I wanted to get away again; go to ground until it was all over. I'd be happy to stay at home, but because people can't bear the thought of someone being on their own at Christmas, I think I could end up feeling pressure. As harsh as it might sound, Darling, I don't want to be with family or friends. My heart is broken. 'Happy Families' it won't be for me. This will be my third Christmas without you and perhaps by now I should be over it (Christmas pain, I mean) but my pain is raw.

That's how I was thinking. I do worry that I'm distancing myself at a time when families get together, but remember I am alone in the desert of my mind.

*****

Tonight I went to the Lions Club of Newbury annual fireworks event at the racecourse. It's close enough that I could have stayed home to watch the display (like you and I used to) but so often when I've seen it from the house I've wished I was there. The fireworks are always fantastic and I know that the Lions spend many thousands of pounds on them every year.

I met several Lions who have known me for a long time. I was asked if I had thought about 'coming back', to which I replied, 'Yes'. And perhaps I will, one day.

The evening was perfect: it was fine, dry and not too cold. The breeze was light and away from the crowd. As I looked around, at a thousand and more faces, I saw many lit up by their mobile phones as people swapped texts or picture messages to confirm what a brilliant firework display it was.

*****

I'm worried about Dennis. I met him at his home this morning and we drove to a village about ten miles away, where he has reserved a small flat. It is in a block of sheltered accommodation and costs £100 a week to rent. Dennis has already paid two weeks' rent, but isn't sure if he is doing the right thing. He currently lives alone in a detached bungalow. If he takes up the flat he will sell the bungalow. It will fund his new tenancy. But it isn't that simple. As I have said to him, this isn't just about moving, this is a massive change to his life. He'll be letting go of the bungalow and his memories there of his darling Betty; and he will have to reduce his belongings down to the bare necessities just to be able to fit into the flat because it is very small. Whether he moves or not, Dennis told me that he was either going to die in the bungalow or in the flat. His decision would govern the rest of his life.

I wanted to help and surely I would, but I cannot say what is for the best because I don't know. I suggested that he write on two pieces of paper all the reasons for choosing one or the other. For example, he might put a big tick in the box for the village because he will have a more active social life. The bungalow might get a tick because of its size and another because it has a garage; the village because he will be able to walk from the flat to the shops.

He admitted to me that the stress of the situation is so bad he thinks it might kill him. I think that, too.

*****

I woke in the very small hours; went to the bathroom; returned to my bed.

'I'm getting a cold,' I muttered to myself.

I had that sensation in my throat that I have just entered the first stage of a virus.

'This'll be two weeks or a fortnight,' I complained.

*****

By jingo, I have not felt this rough for a long time – for years. Whatever is coursing through me is already showing signs of worsening.

I took some more paracetamol and went to bed all afternoon. I lay there with only my mobile phone for company, concerned that I was becoming more ill by the hour and worried that I might not be able to take care of myself. The worst thing of all was the headache. Nothing seemed to bat it away.

*****

It's mid morning on Monday, the start of another working week, and I am still in bed. I spent the whole day in bed yesterday, except for the necessary things like the bathroom, food and fluid, medication and *X Factor*. My head isn't pounding like it was yesterday, but my body feels as though it has been kicked around. I have a dull ache in my lower back and hips.

It was half way through the afternoon before I eventually got up.

*****

I felt better at last. Golly, Darling, whatever that was really knocked me back for a while.

Alec drove Pat and me to the Submarine Museum at Gosport. We had set this up before I fell ill, but today we were three retired men enthusing about conserved wrecks and preserved submarines. It was a great day out and the weather was sunny and mild.

To get to the museum, we had to drive over the bridge at Haslar. It was the bridge right next to Haslar Marina, from where you and I went sailing with friends. You'll remember how I got seasick on that yacht even before we set out.

My own memories came flooding back but, to my pleasant surprise, I did not get upset.

*****

I sent off a cheque for a bulk order of 200 *Bright Lights and Fairy Dust* books. I suppose things are moving on, but progress feels painfully slow.

I also sent a cheque to convert *Bright Lights* into an e-Book. I think it will be good to have that as well as the hardback.

*****

The publishers confirmed today that they received the cheque and, after asking me if I wanted silver or gold lettering on the spine, came back before the end of the day to let me know my 200 books would be delivered in two weeks.

*****

To get through Christmas this year I went to the Isle of Wight. I stayed at Norton Grange, where you and I spent several holidays together. We loved our time there. The place looked just the same and the same chap was still on reception. He seemed not to have changed even after all these years.

My first night was, to say the least, eventful. As I sat down at my table for one in the Castaways Restaurant, I saw there was a bottle of red wine next to my glass. The thoughtful staff had left a complimentary drink for me. They never did that for us. When the waitress came to my table she asked if I would like her to open the bottle. My polite response was in the affirmative and so she pulled the cork from the bottle and poured me the first drink. Things had changed after all, I thought, and for the better. I don't often drink red wine, so this was a treat for me.

My enjoyment was short-lived. Due to some poor handwriting on the ticket on the bottle, the wine on table 73 was actually for table 75, a table set for four, and they had paid for it.

I worked something out with my new neighbours and it was all very relaxed in the end.

Much later in the evening, after the entertainment, I returned to my chalet and sat listening to the radio. The sound of a key being turned in my door gave me a bit of a shock. I opened the door and two women were standing there. I couldn't help thinking, albeit it in a silly way, that Norton Grange was definitely looking after me on my latest visit. But, of course, it was another misunderstanding: they had the right room number but the wrong block and, after apologising, went off to their accommodation.

On Christmas Eve I drove to Newport and mooched around the stores and charity shops. As I walked past Newport Minster in the town centre I heard The Salvation Army playing a beautiful tune. Tears gathered, but I did not let them fall. It was a difficult moment that caught me off guard as once again the reality of my situation hit home.

My third Christmas without you and my pain is no less now than when you died. My heart remains heavy and permanently damaged but – and this is what I want to say on the matter – I have been learning to cope somehow. I've written in the pages of my diary that I must be permitted to put my pain and suffering to one side in order to function and in order to move on with the life I have left. I do know beyond doubt that I must have done that to an extent because here I am at one of our favourite holiday resorts and I feel strong (or stronger, at least). I am holding it all together and, as a matter of fact, I am able to cherish the memories of our times here.

That evening, Norton Grange laid on a minibus to take people to mass. I was surprised at how many fellow Grangers wanted to celebrate and it required two trips for the driver to move everyone waiting in reception. We were among the first to arrive at St. James's Church in Yarmouth. Although it meant we had a long wait before the service began, it gave us an opportunity to sit in one of the front pews. The church continued to fill with worshippers until every last corner of it was crammed.

Two special things happened for me at this midnight mass. The first was that the vicar called out to me in the front row and asked me to read a prayer from the lectionary. The other was that it was my first Christmas at which I took communion.

And I can tell you, Linda, I felt that I was *in* communion and that what was happening to me was so right.

*****

After breakfast on Christmas Day, I went swimming in the heated pool. Swimming with a full stomach wasn't a good idea. As I thrashed around, like a man overboard, I had to put up with the non-stop and perfectly rhythmic swimming of a woman who went from one side of the pool to the other, stopping only once to lift her polarised goggles so that she could see who it was huffing and puffing in her ear as she glided past. I guess she had to put up with me too.

When I got back to my chalet, I showered away the pool chemicals and tried to send a text to Wayne and Sara. I'd left them a voicemail too, but my phone was quiet. I had plenty of bars on my signal indicator, but '*no network*' showing on the screen. The silence was eerie and yet it afforded me the Christmas that I wanted: one without the pressure to call here and call there. I couldn't.

I had lunch and dinner, after which I called Wayne using the payphone in the lobby because I wanted to speak to him before the day expired. As I picked up the handset my mind was cast back to my time in Police College, when I would call home using often a handful and more of silver coins.

Wayne told me that he, Sara, Lola and Darcy had had a tiring Christmas and one that was short on sleep. They were hoping for a better night that night.

I also made a call to Mum and Dad, which seemed to seal my earlier recollections of Police College in my memory.

*****

The next morning I walked to the Needles from the monument on Tennyson Down, a distance of about two and a half miles. It was a walk into wind, during which I was able to watch the ravens along the cliff tops holding themselves aloft on outstretched wings. Then they would draw their wings in and flip over, instantly losing height before recovering from their stall to sit once more on the breeze.

I wonder why a group of ravens is called an unkindness.

On reaching the western tip of the island I used my new contract mobile to take and send a picture of The Needles and the Needles lighthouse. I was merely on one of the many 'tourist' trails, with the rocket testing site behind me and the coastguard station above, but the views were stunning. You and I loved it here.

To go with the picture, I added a text and sent it to Wayne and Sara:

> *Blimey, it sure is windy!*
> *Well, Boxing Day. Another surreal experience. The wind cuts, but it is generally mild – and dry. The Wight Road Runners have run from Freshwater Bay to touch the railings here at The Needles. They're on the way back now.*
> *Me too, but at walking pace. x*

*****

Back in my chalet after the evening's entertainment, I popped a memo into my mobile, making sure it was in long hand rather than in note form. I also made a point of typing it, not using voice recording, because I couldn't make any sense of the last one I had spoken into the device.

> *It's my last night.*
> *I feel 'empowered' I think.*
> *I have met some wonderful people and I have done as much or as little to please myself.*
> *Tears have come.*
> *I have let some flow and held back others. It has been another pilgrimage of love, of meeting*

myself at times as I retrace some of the steps we took together.
I miss you with all my heart, Darling.
I promise I am trying hard to be strong. x

Four

I know I changed after you died.

I began to see things differently, looked for things, for answers, for reasons, in ways I wouldn't have done prior to you becoming ill. And rather than turning away from God, as some people do, I wanted to continue reaching out, hoping that I might gain a greater understanding of the grand order of life and death.

I lean further towards the idea of the existence of a parallel plane to the one in which we live. A spiritual world, a world of faerie. I think of it as one that mostly bobs along without the need to involve us but which, every so often, gives us a nudge, or a sign, or a bit of help when we might not even realise we need it. I think it's why we have 'Wagamama days', when you make the sun shine between dull, rainy days, or when the sky is blue but ought really to be grey. I feel a connection, too, whenever I spot a little white feather, such as might have come from the wings of an angel. I don't try to explain these things, but I know they help me.

Perhaps, for me, this is another view of faith. After all, none of us knows.

Everything I have written to you here has come from my heart, whether it's been just a few words in a day, or whole pages of notes.

I have found it interesting to reflect on how some of my thoughts have changed and some have not. At the same time, I can also see from my own text that there has been a degree of healing.

Some of my ramblings reveal that I have done rather a lot of mumbling and muttering to both myself and to you. This is something that continues. I find it helpful. It makes things real, come alive. Like the writing, it brings you a little closer.

As I have copied my notes and journal entries for you, I have given lots of thought as to how I might draw this to a close. I've covered little more than two years here, but many more have passed now. And, remember, there isn't a time frame.

What I can say, of course, is that I am continuing to put more time behind me. It's still the case that moments of emotional ambush are never far away but, by opening my mind and heart – indeed my very being – to everyone and everything around me, I have had some amazing and enduring experiences. Every day, and with each passing week, month and year, I am nourished and restored by the people and events in my life. I have been given the strength to continue moving forward.

And a belief in life after death.

Five

Those days...

...the phone doesn't ring like it used to and I don't get visitors like I once did.

Is this, I wonder, because everyone else has moved on? Those who have mourned their dear friend Linda have moved forward more quickly than I? For many people, my wife's death was an event. These things happen. Perhaps they think I can get along fine now and that I am over it.

They're wrong. My grief is ongoing. But I know I am better to smile above the clouds than hang my head in a ground-hugging fog.

From the moment you were diagnosed, you and I set out on a new voyage.

For me, that voyage continues.

And you are by my side every step of the way.

I love you, Dolly,

CP

xx

PS: I still have 745 address labels left. These days, it's not often that I write a letter.

Music

I'll Be A Sunbeam	Talbot, Excell	1900
I'll Walk Beside You	Murray, Lockton	1939
How Much Is That Doggie	Bob Merrill	1952
Round Every Corner	Tony Hatch	1965
Three Little Birds	Bob Marley	1980
Hill Street Blues	Mike Post	1981
Ride On	Jimmy MacCarthy	1984
You Are My Life	Chris Page	1995
Yellow	Martin, Buckland, Berryman, Champion	2000
So Do I	Wally Page	2001
Wrong Foot Forward	Allen, Finnegan	2005

Hymns

Praise My Soul The King Of Heaven
The King Of Love My Shepherd Is
Guide Me Oh Thou Great Redeemer
Oh God, Our Help In Ages Past
Give Me Joy In My Heart
All Things Bright And Beautiful

Books

Father Neil McNicholas
A Catholic Approach To Dying
London: Catholic Truth Society 2006

Virginia Ironside
You'll Get Over It
London: Penguin Books 1997

Fiona Murray
Messages From Nature's Guardians
Ribble Press 2009

Lightning Source UK Ltd.
Milton Keynes UK
UKHW040746281118
333066UK00001B/34/P

9 781786 234056